God's Postmarks

Signs God Gives of His Love for Us

Barbara J. Cornelius

God's Postmarks
Signs God Gives of His Love for Us

ISBN 978-0-9883261-7-0
copyright © 2014 Barbara J. Cornelius
All rights reserved

interior design and format Dekie Hicks
cover art and interior illustrations Cody Matthews

ACKNOWLEDGEMENTS

I am very grateful to my husband, Larry Cornelius, for his investment of time and inspiration in the preparation of this book. My words in the chapters of this book are my testimony of how the Lord daily directs my steps, and without Larry's assistance this testimony would have remained unwritten.

I would also like to thank my daughter Jennifer, son-in-law Earl, son Jeff, and daughter-in-law Julie for the Christian witness they have for the Lord and how that blesses our entire family.

My eight grandchildren: Brandon Wyatt, Alyssa Wyatt, Jacie Snipes, Benjamin Snipes, Abigail Cornelius, Jeffrey Cornelius, Robert Cornelius, and Martha Cornelius have drenched my life with joy, and I pray that every day of their lives they will carry God's light inside of them and call forth God's kingdom.

I am grateful to my cousin Mary Dell Memering, my incredible friend Gloria Parker, and my sister-in-law Lana Frady. Their prayers for me have been deeply felt and their encouragement and love have blessed my life. They have inspired me to ask the Lord to order my steps that I might do the same for others.

Most of all, I seek to give my Lord Jesus honor and glory for what He has meant to my life. Despite all my many failings, He has made His presence known to me since I was a child. I praise God for letting me write about some of the signs He gives to reveal His work on behalf of believers. Praise Him! Praise Him!

Table of Contents

God's Postmarks

Introduction

*I*had just finished writing a chapter for this book when my husband looked through the sliding-glass doors in our vacation home in the mountains and saw a huge, magnificent rainbow hovering close to our two-stories-high deck. It was the largest and closest rainbow we had ever witnessed! Larry and I felt the Lord had given us a special postmark of His blessing on the message of this book: Daily He provides us with signs He is "on the job" and is performing His work on our behalf.

Reading in Scripture about John and Ezekiel's experiences in the throne room has inspired me to believe rainbows are one of God's trademarks, which I call "postmarks." Postmarks on letters, postcards, and packages indicate they were delivered under the care of the postal service. I believe God is giving us these kinds of signs in amazing, beautiful, and sometimes subtle ways every day so we will know we are under His care. If we pay attention and look for such signs, we open ourselves to opportunities to be blessed by our caring, loving God and experience encouragement for the trials and challenges of our daily living.

Often we become discouraged and believe our prayers are going into a vacuum instead of reaching the hands of God. We accept the belief that what has been true in the past will always be true today and will bring defeat in our present circumstances. This belief is a lie from the enemy, and the truth is, God is always providing encouraging signs of His presence in all situations as they evolve in our daily living.

Recently I was required to have blood specimens taken three times in one week, and I am sure only a "wimp" like me would complain about such a minor ordeal. However, for the past several years, only veins in my hands could be used for blood sampling. The technicians would probe and slap my arms in attempts to locate a vein to draw blood, and then tell me the veins in my arms were just too deep to be used. Recently, after the first blood sample was drawn, I experienced a badly bruised hand and dreaded going again to the lab.

Before my next visit to the lab, I called my dear sister-in-law, Lana, and best friend, Gloria, to pray for me. While I was sitting in my chair, the technician entered the pertinent data, and I watched her face, which was missing a frown of deep concentration, but instead had a quiet, joyful appearance. This second experience was miraculous to me because the technician could see a vein in my arm before she sat down, and I barely felt the prick of the needle. However, after the results were known, I was sent back to the lab for the third time. I told my sister-in-law I knew her prayers for this visit would be in the lab even before I arrived.

When I entered the lab that following morning the same technician "happened" to be in the office, and I asked her if she would please draw the blood. I experienced the same miracle I had had with her two days earlier. Both experiences revealed she is a strong believer and God put her in place to be a testimony to His caring nature for His children. I felt exhilarated when I left because my Father had shown me He was watching over me through the hands of a skillful lab technician. What I had experienced in the past was not a part of my present situation, and He was letting me know through an otherwise unpleasant experience.

Take a close look every day at the sky and your surroundings, your circumstances, your "coincidences" and God's Word, and you will see He is looking out for you and is very much present in your life. Do not believe Satan's falsehood that nothing will change when failure and discouragement haunt you. Don't miss finding the living God as He permeates your space today. He is standing right beside you holding you tightly in His hands. Praise the living God!

～

May all people who read this book receive spiritual blessings and may God's kingdom be called forth in their lives.

～

Matthew 18:1-4*

At that time the disciples came to Jesus, saying "Who is the greatest in the kingdom of heaven?" And calling to him a child, he put him in the midst of them and said, "Truly, I say to you, unless you turn and become like children, you will never enter the kingdom of heaven. Whoever humbles himself like this child is the greatest in the kingdom of heaven."

*ESV

CHAPTER ONE
God's Postmarks in Children's Voices

I sat down in a comfortable chair in the lobby of a bank to wait for assistance when a three-year-old blonde boy eagerly came and sat near my feet. He talked non-stop giving me all kinds of unsolicited information about his fourth birthday party scheduled for the following week, his favorite toys, video games, television programs, etc. I had no clue where his parents were, but he seemed to feel very secure with his surroundings. Suddenly he stopped and looked at me with a large grin and said, "My father says that I will die someday." His radiant face showed no signs of illness, and he demonstrated absolutely no anxiety about the words he had just offered to me. He continued on with his delightful chatter to other topics, but his words stunned me.

I actually felt reluctant to leave this wonderful source of joy and entertainment after my name was called. Seeing me leave, he then turned his attention to another adult who had just recently sat in one of the chairs. When I entered the bank attendant's office, I looked at the large window behind his desk and saw something unusual. I know it was placed there to underscore that I was having a "God Moment." In the early morning condensation on the window, someone from the outside who had been passing by had drawn a small stick figure. God was not only creating something special for me, He was "winking at me!"

Over sixty years ago, a few months before my blonde-headed, blue-eyed nine-year-old brother, Bobby, passed away, my mother had told him that he would be going to a medical center about sixty miles away for some diagnostic tests.

This precious little boy said, "It's too late for me to be healed." How did Bobby know his time to die was coming so soon? My mother's aching heart could not receive the message that her only son would soon be leaving this earth, but I believe the Lord was slowly preparing her. He knows the burden this kind of heartbreaking loss brings because He sacrificed His only son.

In my years as an elementary and middle school teacher, mother of two, and grandmother of eight, I have marveled at some of the profound things that come out of the mouths of small children when they are having an incredibly sweet moment. On one occasion, my then two-year-old granddaughter, Martha, came scampering up the steps of our front porch greeting me with an urgent request. With sparkling eyes she said, "Meemaw, I want to hold you!" My first reaction was to laugh as my practical nature took over. Martha didn't know she was literally saying she wanted to place a large adult in her lap. She just knew she wanted me to take her in my arms and love up on her. Perhaps words such as these "turned inside out" by a child are simply a message from the Lord. Maybe He is saying that when you hear those words, remember that I, the living God, want to hold you and love you through the warm, soft touch of a child in your lap!

Children don't have to ponder when and where to share their thoughts and opinions. When they are surrounded by parents, family, and friends who give witness to the Lord, they absorb this testimony and grow in knowledge of Him. They share their minds effortlessly and without any interference from the world. My seven-year-old granddaughter, Abigail, has been reciting Scripture since she was three years old. She takes great delight in telling family and total strangers about Jesus.

My oldest grandson, Brandon, at the age of seven, surprised the entire family when he asked if he could say the family prayer before our meal in a local restaurant. We were amazed by the mature prayer spoken from his young lips. When I shared this story with a friend, she said "My four-year-old grandson has been doing the same thing. I believe it is a spiritual gift." This comment reminded me of a story I read about a young teenager who had been in a horrific car accident and suffered terrible brain damage. She could barely utter an intelligent word and her short-term memory was severely damaged. However, at times she supernaturally prayed coherently and recited large passages of Scripture. The family's explanation was that the Holy Spirit was speaking through her during those times. Sometimes our Lord's Spirit speaks through us in dramatic, miraculous ways as was the case with this young woman. At other times, He communicates during quiet, miraculous moments through the mouths of small children.

Today the urgency to share the message of salvation is being preached in churches, spoken of in Bible study classes, discussed among Christians around the world, and most importantly written in the hearts of believers. Death will claim us someday. Will we leave this earth knowing we have answered God's call for our testimony? Have we shared God's Word with others, and when we arrive in heaven, will there be anyone there because we were blessed to have the Lord use our mouths for testimony? Did we identify our mission field everywhere the Lord left His footprints for us? Children often seem to get to the point of what is important spiritually sooner than adults. Somehow they seem to have God's ear, and He uses their sweet voices to spread the Good News of His work. Let us follow their example.

Have the heart of a child and allow the message of salvation to spring from your mouth. Pray to be anointed by the Holy Spirit so the power of the living God can reign in your spirit. Be like a joyful child who wants everyone to join him at the grand party that will be given when we all celebrate being with our Father in heaven!

Have the heart of a child and let the message of salvation come freely from your spirit.

Genesis 9: 12- 13

And God said, "I am giving you a sign as evidence of my eternal covenant with you and all living creatures. I have placed my rainbow in the clouds. It is the sign of my permanent promise to you and to all of the earth."

Ezekiel 1:1, 1:28*

1:1...the heavens were opened and I saw visions of God.

1:28 Like the appearance of a rainbow in a cloud on a rainy day, so was the brightness all around it. This was the appearance of the likeness of the glory of the LORD.

Revelation 4: 2- 3*

Immediately I was in the Spirit: and behold, a throne set in heaven, and One sat on the throne. And He who sat there was like a jasper and a sardius stone in appearance: and there was a rainbow around the throne, in appearance like an emerald.

*NKJV

CHAPTER TWO

One of God's Favorite Postmarks: Rainbows

*T*he broken-hearted young man peered at the sky and couldn't believe his eyes—a huge rainbow had suddenly appeared. The young lady he had loved and pursued had chosen someone else. Several of his supportive friends stood silently around him with tears in their eyes as they observed the sight. The young man had lost his beloved mother a short time ago, and her dying words to her son were: "When you see a rainbow in the sky, it is a sign from me that I am with you." The sight of this rainbow renewed the memory of her words and brought him the comfort his soul craved. Surely, God had synchronized that moment in time for all who were present to highlight one of His favorite postmarks.

Rainbows have a special way of lifting hurting spirits and bringing surprising joy to many. I have been delighted many times upon discovering "accidental" rainbows in my own home. Sometimes when sunlight has come at just the right angle through a window, they have suddenly appeared. I never know when these unexpected visual treats are going to show up, and I always savor the experience of finding them. Truly, they are one of God's beautiful "coincidences."

Sometimes when I see rainbows, I am reminded of years

past when I led my sixth grade science students in fun-filled moments of discovery about light on planet Earth. They delighted in seeing the spectrum of light by looking through spectroscopes and prisms and blowing bubbles on their desks. They loved memorizing and reciting the seven colors that comprise white light by using the name of ROY G BIV (red, orange, yellow, green, blue, indigo, and violet) and enthusiastically shouting out the colors as they recognized them in bubbles. As a long-time educator I have always believed that seeing is often imperative to knowing, and so I taped a cardboard circle containing the seven individual colors to a beater of an electric mixer. As it rotated, the colors blended into a whitish color. Motivated to provide them with a really unique learning experience, I also put my students inside bubbles. They excitedly waited for their turns to be enclosed in a gigantic bubble by standing in a wading pool and having me raise a hula hoop of bubble solution over each of them. Joy abounded in my classroom!

I wanted my students to be gifted with the realization of the incredible miracle our Creator presented to the world when He spoke light into existence at the beginning of creation. The power and majesty of our heavenly Father is revealed to us in Genesis1:3: "And God said, 'Let there be light,' and there was light. God saw that the light was good, and He separated the light from the darkness." With this amazing illumination from the hand of the living God came hidden rainbows wherever man places his feet.

Learning a scientific explanation for the formation of rainbows was a part of our classroom activities. We would discuss how they are produced by the bending of light as it travels through certain materials, and how each color, traveling at a different speed, causes it to be seen individually. Light is a precious gift from God with many beautiful components. We recognize these components only when we look for them.

John records in chapter four of the Book of Revelation his spirit journey to heaven. He vividly describes his vision of going through an open door and seeing the majestic living God presiding on His throne which is surrounded by His glory and a rainbow. When I read this Scripture, I love to visualize the light of God radiating from His throne and seeing it stream through His glory and be refracted into the most beautiful rainbow that could ever be seen in heaven or on Earth. What John saw had to be so breath-taking in its beauty that no words could possibly describe it. Surely this sight must have thrilled him to his very core! Pure joy radiates throughout my spirit every time I think about that vision!

The rainbow in the throne room is also described in the Old Testament in Chapter One of the Book of Ezekiel. Ezekiel dramatically tells of his vision of heaven being opened up and his viewing God on His throne. He says, "Like the appearance of a rainbow in the clouds on a rainy day, so was the radiance around him." He gives us a stunning, beautiful picture of the rainbow that encircles the throne of our living God!

In the Book of Genesis God decides to share His rainbow with the world. He tells Noah after the great flood that He is placing His rainbow in the sky as a promise to him and all of God's people that He will never again destroy the earth with a flood. Notice, Scripture doesn't say *a* rainbow. It says *His* rainbow! It seems so like our awesome God that He would take something so sacred in His throne room and duplicate it in the sky for us to see and recognize how much He treasures us! Wow!

Sometimes, these rainbows come in the midst of deep sorrow and grief. I can still hear my friend crying a few years ago as she fervently prayed, "Dear Father, please heal my beloved mother. I am in desperate need of You. Please give me a sign that You are really hearing my prayer." Tragically, her mother died a few months later, but the day of the funeral God gave her the sign she had requested. A huge rainbow appeared in the sky directly over the funeral home. He had taken her mother to heaven where she was healed.

Recently, I had an opportunity to speak to a women's group at a church in a town an hour away from my home. I knew only one of the women who would be there, and had actually met her on only a couple of occasions. I knew the Lord had given me a great opportunity to give my testimony, and I didn't want to fail Him by being focused on my speech instead of His divine purpose for the evening. I asked some friends to support me in prayer, and they responded by praying during the time they believed I would actually be speaking.

Later, after I had given my talk, one of the ladies in attendance handed me a note. She had written that during the last few minutes of my speech a rainbow appeared above my head. I hesitated to share her comments with others lest they might think I thought I was special in some way. The Lord, however, revealed to me that I needed to tell my supportive prayer friends of His postmark on the event to let them know what He had done! He had given them a sign that He had answered their prayers!

Indeed, it is important that we recognize the inconspicuous, quiet times that present us with opportunities to give testimony for the Lord. My granddaughter, Alyssa, recently experienced a very tough day at school and spent most of the evening in tears. Her mother, my daughter Jennifer, told her to go outside and look at the darkening sky. There in the midst of the fading evening light she saw a beautiful rainbow piercing through some large white clouds. She took a picture of this beautiful sight and posted it on Facebook with the caption: "God spoke to me tonight." Over two hundred people on this site were witness to her testimony about God's postmark to her in the midst of her distress.

Ponder this thought. Every time we walk into a location with illumination supplied by sunlight or a source of artificial light, we are walking in the presence of God's rainbows. Sometimes we discover them when a piece of glass in our home breaks up the light. On other occasions we can spot them when He supernaturally places them in an unusual location right in front of us. Occasionally, we can celebrate rainbows when they appear in the sky after the rain has drenched the earth. Whether or not we observe God's colorful masterpieces, they are always around us to signify His presence.

Seek to remove yourself from all the distractions that surround you and stop to receive the gift of God' s presence. He is always there in all His glory! Remember the promise of a new earth and new heaven as it is described for the final chapter of the universe in the Book of Revelation.

The sun will disappear for it will no longer be needed. God is light and the Holy City will be full of His light and glory. We will then be in the presence of the living God who is the Creator of all our rainbows. Praise Him! Praise Him!

Seek to remove yourself from distractions that keep you from being in God's presence. He is waiting for you in all of His glory!

Isaiah 58:8

"If you do these things, your salvation will come like the dawn. Yes, your healing will come quickly. Your godliness will lead you forward, and the glory of the LORD will protect you from behind."

CHAPTER THREE

God's Postmark of Human Angels in Our Midst

*S*omething about Ginger's countenance draws me to her when I enter the grocery store. She is quiet and unassuming, and her eyes sparkle with light. She prepares the demonstration meals at various times during the week and creates an atmosphere of quiet joy whenever she's there. Many seem not to notice her, but I see her glowing face soon after I enter the store.

Ginger calls me by name when she sees me, even though we've never met outside the store! I feel as if I am seeing a long-time friend when she greets me. Her friendliness permeates the store, and I always feel blessed as I shop after I have seen her. Even though our lives mingle only in a casual way, we have great favor with each other as if we've shared many pleasant experiences.

Ginger seems to be a "calling card" for this store. She performs her duties in a quiet, conscientious manner, and I believe she makes the living God smile as she projects His grace into her surroundings. Even though our conversations are brief, I sometimes stop to say a short prayer over her. To support herself, she holds down several jobs. She once commented about her concern for a very elderly lady she stays with a few days a month. When I shared with her that she could ask God to "wrap His arms around her friend" in His love, she tearfully told me, "I just felt the Holy Spirit wash over me." Ginger is one of God's human angels I have been blessed to meet in many places at various times in my life. She and I share a connection made by the Holy Spirit.

Over and over the Lord will connect His people in these kinds of ways so they can receive numerous blessings from His hand. When my daughter, Jennifer, was pregnant with her second child, she made five trips to the emergency room with premature labor pains. At the time, she was going through the trauma of divorce and had heightened anxiety about this pregnancy since her first child had been born almost seven weeks early. On one of those visits she met a nurse named Sarah who graciously shared her faith. Her soothing words eased my daughter's fear and gave her the strength she needed during that stressful time.

It has now been fourteen years since the birth of Jennifer's second child. During this time I have seen her express the same compassion toward others who came her way. I believe Sarah's seeds of faith have blessed the lives of hundreds of patients who God put in her path. She certainly was a visible angel of light for our family when we desperately needed her words of encouragement.

God frequently puts people like Ginger and Sarah in our paths. Somehow we seem to be connected to these individuals with an invisible thread. Certain people just seem to have the right words and advice for others in troubling situations. They may be found in ordinary places such as stores which sell groceries, appliances, or even hardware supplies.

You may also see evidence of this invisible thread when people are motivated to offer assistance to meet your needs. Years ago, when I was trying to assemble "home-made" science kits for other teachers without much available financial support from the school system, I asked for help from Michael, a man I knew from church who worked at a local hardware store. Having been an elementary and middle-school classroom teacher for many years before I became a science resource teacher for the county, I knew which materials teachers needed to perform hands-on science activities in their classrooms. I have always believed that when children experience engaging science activities with their teachers, they make more connections with the creative world around them. God speaks silently to all of us when we notice and appreciate what He has done in creation.

I frequently would go into Michael's store and tell him what materials I was trying to duplicate from a science catalog, and he would make suggestions and help me identify them in his store or catalogs. We made a very good team, and the hundreds of science kits distributed to teachers had his imprint on them. God multiplied Michael's efforts for hundreds of students and even though his words of testimony were not heard by them, the students were blessed by his faith manifested in his deeds. God had connected the two of us in a way that blessed many children.

Amazingly God sometimes gives me favor with people I have never seen before. Recently, my seven-year-old granddaughter, Jacie, asked me why so many people seem to know me. She sees God's favor on me with people in many different places as they wave and speak to me as if we are long-time friends. Conversation flows easily, smiles are exchanged, and brief, but meaningful words about the Lord are shared.

I frequently say, "Have a blessed day!" to people I meet and watch their reactions. Oftentimes a thread of recognition is woven in the face of the person who hears those words. Most people smile back and repeat words of equal affirmation as we experience God's favor between us. I also pray for strangers I meet throughout my day as the Holy Spirit prompts me. I feel the positive energy of the Holy Spirit deep inside my own spirit as I pray and experience favor from someone I will never really know.

Many people who come our way and bless us with kind words and deeds are purposely put in our paths by our living God. He also places people in our midst who need those very things from us. He has woven a connecting fiber throughout our spirits which draws us to each other. Ponder the times when you were trying to comfort someone, and words of inspiration, absent only moments before you spoke, just seemed to come to you. I believe this is the Holy Spirit working through us in these situations.

Are you aware that nearly every day God gives us circumstances to manifest His love in the lives of others? Many times we might not ever know how the Lord has used us, but we certainly are thankful when we recognize someone who knows Him and has touched our own lives. Praise God today for those who have touched your life and seek opportunities to bless others in His name! Give Him the honor and glory!

Every day look for chances to bless others in the name of Jesus.

Ephesians 1:18-20

I pray that your hearts will be flooded with light so that you can understand the confident hope he has given to those he has called—his holy people who are his rich and glorious inheritance. I also pray that you will understand the incredible greatness of God's power for us who believe him. This is the same mighty power that raised Christ from the dead and seated him in the place of honor at God's right hand in the heavenly realms.

CHAPTER FOUR

God's Postmarks: Spoken Words of Love

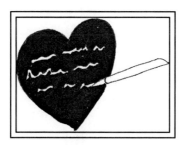

$\mathcal{T}$he sight of the one pound, fifteen ounce baby took her breath away. The grandmother's anxiety-laden eyes took in every feature of her tiny grandson. He had been born fifteen weeks early, but the doctors had told the family that the baby had a seventy-five percent chance of surviving. The family realized they would in all probability face many hurdles and stressful days in the months ahead, but they also knew that these would be addressed with one "faith step" at a time. They had seen the hand of God touch their family on many miraculous occasions in the past, and they trusted Him with this baby boy's future.

The grandmother fell in love with her cherished grandson in those first few moments. Her own cherished mother, a woman of great faith, had died just a few months earlier, and her aching heart felt a surge of joy that had been hopelessly missing during that time of profound grief.

The parents also had felt an urgent need to connect with their son and let him know who they were. In the twenty-four hours since he had been born, they persistently spoke to the baby saying, "Please open your little eyes so that we can see you!" Yet the baby's eyes remained closed.

Inspired words tumbled from the grandmother's mouth as she had her first conversation with the baby. "Bryson, I am your grandmother and I love you so very much. I want you to know that God sent His angels to be with me at all times, and I always feel their presence. I asked my angels to surround you and protect you as they have protected me. I have even asked them to ask their 'angel buddies' to join them in this mission."

At the sound of the grandmother's words, miraculously the baby's tiny eyes opened. His beautiful, bright eyes seemed to be saying that he had heard the message. God was giving his family a postmark to let them know that He was on the job protecting this child's future. A testimony for the world was being written in his little spirit.

At times words of love spoken to someone can have a profound effect on their spirit that cannot be observed by human eyes. Almost thirty years ago our family drove over five hundred miles for a family reunion which included my husband's parents. When it came time for us to leave and return home, our daughter, who was ten years old at the time, approached her grandfather. Without any adult prompting she spoke words to him that he never said to others, "I love you!" Although she did not receive a response, his countenance seemed to change and his face seemed to relax as if he had received pleasure upon hearing those words.

I can only imagine the surprise he felt as he heard the unexpected words. He had many challenging habits and had always been a difficult person to be around. At that time I could not remember being in his presence and hearing anyone speak the words "I love you!"

Over the next few years my father-in-law's health deteriorated and several visits occurred in hospital rooms. The words of love that had been spoken by a child began to be repeated by other family members whenever they made those visits. No response was ever given, but many of us felt blessed by just delivering the message. God provided encouragement for us in the midst of the silence.

When my father-in-law died, we all grieved that he had never made a known profession of faith. Over the years he always refused invitations to attend any church services. Even in his last days he would not allow the family to invite a pastor to come and speak with him. Strangely though, on many Sunday mornings he could be seen in his living room listening to ministers' sermons on television. Still, his failure to speak words of faith caused great heartache for the family. We had no outward sign that my father-in-law's eternal home was with the Lord.

It has now been sixteen years since his death. Two years after his passing I had the only dream about him I have ever had. It was one of the most vivid and real dreams I have ever experienced. I saw my father-in-law seated beside a riverbank in heaven. He was bathed in light, and love seemed to radiate from his entire body. He looked young, healthy and better than I had ever seen him appear in life. I was there with him, and as I approached him, he arose and silently acknowledged me. The dream ended with the two of us walking together along the riverbank to an unknown destination in heaven. When I awoke, I felt that someday when I arrive at my heavenly home, my father-in-law will be one of the people there to greet me.

Shortly after I shared this dream with my husband, he told me something I did not know. The river had always been his father's most favorite place to relax. He was always happiest when he was able to spend time there. Experiencing that dream and sharing it with family members gave birth in our spirits to the hope we will see him again when we all go home to be with the Lord.

Perhaps words of love spoken to him over the years generated a spark in his spirit just as my friend's words had for her tiny premature grandson. The baby opened his eyes in response to hearing love expressed to him. I believe it is possible the same thing happened to my father-in-law. Possibly in his last days, words of love that had been incorporated into his spirit, allowed him to hear the Lord's voice. I believe angels were at his side when he was born, and they were also there in his last moments. They were there urging him to respond to the Lord's invitation before he took his last breath and left this earth. I know many prayers for him were lifted up over the years to keep him close to the Lord's presence, and perhaps those prayers kept angels at his side to escort him home.

There are many times in our lives when we have opportunities to allow our lips to be used by the Lord to encourage, love, and bring light into the lives of others. We are made in the image of the living God! When we walk in faith and experience, His Holy Spirit resides in us. His words also dwell in us to empower us to make eternal connections on behalf of the lost.

Have you used your words today to encourage someone who needs them to open their eyes to God's light? Have you shared words of faith and love with a person whose eyes seem to be closed to God's message? Pray for the eyes of your own heart to be opened so that you can see the opportunities the Lord provides to bless others. Will you let the Lord use you to be a "postmark" so that His message about salvation can bless others? I believe speaking the words "I love you" with your heart blesses your very own soul and brings pleasure to God as He says "That is my beloved child!" Pray for God to anoint your mouth so that He can use you to reach others!

Bless others with words of love and faith and receive blessings yourself.

Isaiah 42:16-17*

"I will lead the blind in a way that they do not know, in paths that they have not known I will guide them. I will turn the darkness before them into light, the rough places into level ground. These are the things I will do, and I do not forsake them."

Jeremiah 33:3*

"Call to me and I will answer you, and will tell you great and hidden things that you have not known."

John 8:12

Jesus said to the people, "I am the light of the world. If you follow me, you won't be stumbling through the darkness, because you will have the light that leads to life."

*ESV

CHAPTER FIVE

Postmark in the Dark: The Shepherd's Voice Penetrates Darkness

$\mathcal{T}$wenty-eight men had just arrived at a meeting room located on the fifth floor of the newly remodeled section of the building. They had recently flown in from across the country for a week-long management course entitled "Defense Policy in the 21st Century." This was their first visit to this location and they were all unfamiliar with the large building and its unique design.

Suddenly a large blast shook the entire room. Several of the panels from the suspended ceiling fell to the floor, and the light fixture in the middle of the room came crashing down on the conference table. Smoke immediately began filling the room from the other light fixtures and the vents in the ceiling. Lights were knocked out instantly, and the emergency lights and sprinkler system were also disabled. Everything was engulfed in blackness, and dense smoke and dust began filling the room. It was later learned that this meeting room was located just above the impact area where the left wing of a plane, still connected to its fuselage, had crashed. The occupants of the room were only fifty feet from ground zero of where the plane had entered the building.

The building was the Pentagon in Washington, D.C., and the date was September 11, 2001. The men attending this meeting stepped out into the hall to find it darkened and filled with smoke which lingered from their heads to the ceiling. Their pulses quickened as they struggled to breathe, and they realized they had no clue how to safely proceed in their unfamiliar surroundings. One of the men opened the stairwell door which was directly to their right outside the conference room only to discover the stairs had been demolished and thick, black smoke had filled the area.

Some of the men headed down another hallway to the left where a group of Pentagon employees informed them that the stairwell there was blocked. It had only been about two minutes since the explosion, and the smoke was so thick that they could not see the person in front of them. One of the men later said, "The smell of the smoke was nothing like a campfire, nothing like burning plastic, and nothing like gas, kerosene, or other burning fuels. The odor was like that of a TNT explosion." They were forced to cover their mouths and noses with their jackets, shirtsleeves, or other available items to prevent smoke inhalation. The men began to "duck-walk" in a single line trying to keep as low as possible to stay underneath the smoke. They headed in another direction advancing only a short distance when they made a startling discovery—the floor had sunk down about eighteen inches!

The men continued their cautious advance through the smoke-filled hallway dodging light fixtures and other debris which had fallen to the floor. Their breathing became even more labored as they dealt with the dense smoke which drenched their clothing and stung their eyes. In deafening moments of silence they experienced an adrenaline rush of fear as they began to worry whether or not they would reach safety and see their families again. At least one of the men said a short, silent prayer, "Dear God, please keep us safe!"

The silence was broken by the voice of a man who would later be identified as a security guard yelling, "Grab on to the person ahead of you and keep walking in my direction. You will see light when you reach me!" One of the men later said, "When I reached out to grab the person ahead of me, I found no one within reach. I felt someone behind me grab my coat, but there was no one for me to follow." He was leading the people behind him with no one in front of him to guide the way for him! In his desperation, he called out to the security guard, "Keep talking so I can follow your voice." The guard urged him to find the wall and follow it, but panic momentarily set in when he could not immediately reach the wall. With no other choice, he kept moving through the darkness focusing only on the man's voice which became his anchor.

The guard continued to lead the men with the sound of his voice, promising them they would soon leave the darkness. It seemed like an eternity even though it was probably only a short period of time, when they began to see ahead of them some rays of light and the security official who had been guiding them. The voice in the dark brought them to where they could see a route to safety.

The men continued to rush down the next corridor which was lit, and the smoke seemed to diminish. They quickly went down several sets of escalators to the ground level where they exited the building. Once they were a safe distance away from the building, they stopped to determine if everyone had escaped. Remarkably, the whole group was able to stay calm and collected and exit the building without injury- all within a period of about twenty minutes. One of them later recalled with great emotion, "The security guard was an angel of God sent to lead us through the valley of the shadow of death to a place of light and life". Indeed, the area of the building where they had struggled to find a way to keep their lives, collapsed only thirty minutes later. The voice of The Shepherd heard through the security guard's mouth, called them to their future which He held in His hands.

Altogether, over three thousand lives were lost on September 11, 2001 at the Pentagon, at the World Trade Center, and in the four hijacked planes. Still these men at the Pentagon were guided to safety by a voice that many of them felt came from the Lord. We will never know how many people heard His voice that day as they were guided to safety or how many experienced their last moments on earth with His voice resonating in their spirits. We cannot understand on this side of eternity why our omnipotent God sent His divine assistance to the twenty-eight men in this story and not to the others that perished that day. We do know that their accounting of a miraculous survival brought forth a testimony for them to share with the world.

This story is very personal to me because it was told to me by my nephew who was one of the men who struggled to find his way through the devastation. On many occasions over the years he has spoken about his miraculous escape at the Pentagon on that historic day. His testimony has given the Lord much glory and honor, as have the testimonies of many other believers who experienced His presence on that day.

I believe these men at the Pentagon recognizing the Lord's voice through the security guard's words was a postmark to the world. Sometimes the hopelessness of darkness is not on the outside of people, but dwells inside their spirits and minds. God is telling us to listen for Him when we find ourselves in peril and follow Him into the light.

Do you find yourself walking in darkness because of some fright-ening circumstances in your own life? Do you yearn to hear The Shepherd's voice to guide your steps? His voice resonates through-out every verse of His Word. Read your Bible, pray for His guid-ance and worship the Lord with praise and thanksgiving. He will answer you. He will lead you from the frightening situation that threatens to swallow up your life and into the light of His glorious presence. Listen for Him!

Walk toward God's light by listening to His voice as it resonates through His Word.

1 Chronicles 9: 22- 27*

Altogether, those chosen to be gatekeepers at the thresholds numbered 212. They were registered by genealogy in their villages. The gatekeepers had been assigned to their positions of trust by David and Samuel the seer. They and their descendants were in charge of guarding the gates of the house of the LORD—the house called the Tent. The gatekeepers were on the four sides: east, west, north, and south. Their brothers in their villages had to come from time to time and share their duties for seven-day periods. But the four principal gatekeepers, who were Levites, were entrusted with the responsibility for the rooms and treasures in the house of God. They would spend the night stationed around the house of God, because they had to guard it; and they had charge of the key for opening it each morning.

*NIV

CHAPTER SIX

God's Postmarks: His Gatekeepers

I will never forget her. She was the "gatekeeper" for the rehabilitation center where my elderly mother was sent after suffering a fractured hip. Many visitors, including me, gave her that title because whenever we entered the building through the front door, she seemed to be there sitting quietly in her wheelchair. I began to depend on seeing her and talking to her when I entered and exited the center. Somehow seeing her made me feel happier and more peaceful. If for some reason she was not there, I felt compelled to seek her out.

This very special lady seemed to engender a sweet presence that radiated throughout the building. Something remarkable, but unseen permeated the entire facility. It was as if invisible angels were there to watch over the patients. Even when the staff was overwhelmed with the needs and demands of so many patients, I noticed something special in the eyes of many of them. They treated the precious souls entrusted to them with respect, patience, and even love. One day while I was visiting, I heard one of the staff say to the "gatekeeper", "We love you!" I believe this lady was surrounded by angels, and that she was a special messenger for the living God. I am certain her presence brought a blessing to every person in the center. Sometimes, I would say to her before leaving, "May the angels sleep with you

35

tonight!" Her eyes would light up with joy as if she knew they were already doing just that.

This very special lady had experienced some physical changes which had affected her speech and mobility and had created a need for her to be a patient at the center. Had she not suffered these challenges, I would never have met her. I will always be grateful that I was blessed by the gift of her presence.

Our conversations consisted of just a few words, but I could see the light of Jesus dwelling in her eyes. I began bringing her small gifts to let her know how much seeing her blessed me. One day I brought her one of the inexpensive, multi-colored glass crosses I had given to the women in a Bible study I was leading. I had sent some of these same crosses to my sister-in-law for a women's Christian conference hosted by her church in another state. I told my new friend, "One hundred and forty women in the state of Georgia and Indiana are wearing these crosses, and now you are one of us!" Before I left that day, I saw her proudly wearing her cross and I could tell by her countenance she knew without a doubt she was the daughter of The King.

I wanted her to have the cross to remind her how mighty she was for the Lord. She was revealing to me that she already knew! Something stirred in my spirit every time I saw her. I felt hope, confidence, and even joy for the future surging through me when the final day came for me to visit and take my mother back to her own home. Through the weakness of the gatekeeper, the strength of the living God was seen vividly. No believer could miss seeing Him when they saw her. Our God sent His Son because we were broken and needed His healing hand. Without recognizing our brokenness, we would never truly know of our profound need for our Savior. One of God's postmarks of His presence resided with this lovely lady.

Gatekeepers are written about in several places in the Bible. 1 Chronicles, Chapter 9:17-34 describes the gatekeepers as being assigned to their positions of trust by David and Samuel the seer. Gatekeepers were a select group of anointed people who were required to possess the highest levels of reliability, honesty, and trustworthiness. They and their descendants were in charge of guarding the gates of the house of the LORD. They guarded the four main entrances to the temple and opened the gates each morning for those who wanted to worship. They were charged with preparing offerings and protecting the treasures of the temple. They made sure that unclean things did not enter and defile the temple.

Today's gatekeepers, like my needy friend, may even appear in unexpected places such as a rehabilitation center. Take time to notice them and speak to them. Perhaps they are there to give you a blessed encounter you will never forget as the Lord uses both of you to experience His light and touch. On any given day it could be any of us who resides in a situation that presents a profound burden. It is at this place in a believer's life journey that the Lord offers us an opportunity to be used us as a gatekeeper of faith for others. Pray for courage and wisdom to recognize those times in your life where you may magnify the Lord and let His strength be recognized in your weakness. We are then in an anointed position through which the Holy Spirit can touch the lives of others so that they may someday walk through the gate of eternal life.

Someday my gatekeeper friend and I will be in our heavenly home with our Father. In the midst of all the reunions I will experience, I look forward to seeing her when we both are completely new and restored by God's light and grace. All of our earthly woes and tears will be completely removed from us, and there will be others there with us because of the way God was able to use her. I know I will meet many, many others like her who were gatekeepers for the Lord.

Be watchful for the gatekeepers you meet when you are busy in your daily activities. You may fail to recognize them as you see them in their roles of service in churches, restaurants, stores, hospitals, doctor offices, schools, etc. Many of these servants have been placed there to bless God's treasure- people who come their way at an entry way. Pray that you will not miss any opportunities to recognize them and also bless them in return. Praise God for all the gatekeepers He places in the paths of His people! May much honor and glory be given to Him!

Bless the gatekeepers God places in your path and give honor and glory to Him.

Deuteronomy 31:6

So be strong and courageous! Do not be afraid and do not panic before them. For the LORD your God will personally go ahead of you. He will neither fail you nor abandon you.

Psalm 31:24

So be strong and courageous, all you who put your hope in the LORD!

CHAPTER SEVEN

Postmarks That Help You Practice Your Courage

"Jcan't! I can't!" my distraught three-year-old grand-daughter wailed as she stood in front of the carousel. I tried to comfort her as she struggled with what she wanted to do and what her lack of courage was preventing her from doing. She had been so excited when we first discovered the merry-go-round in the spacious open area in front of some of the stores at our local mall. She couldn't wait to ride the horses with her five-year old brother. He had no problem mounting them and riding as many times as I would allow. Alyssa, how-ever, as desperately as she wanted to ride the one black horse, could not set foot near the carousel. I offered to ride with her and hold her, but her fear was insurmountable.

Every time we visited the mall, she would look at the horses and say, "I want to ride the black horse, but I can't." Indeed, the previous Christmas we had stood in a long line to get her pic-ture taken with Santa Claus and just before it was her turn, the child in front of us began to sob as she was lead over to Santa. Alyssa turned to me and said, "I'm not going to do that!" Yet, when her turn came, the tears came flooding down her cheeks, and we had to retreat to "safety." She wanted to put her fear aside, but she just couldn't bring herself to do it!

After many false starts to the carousel on our visits to the mall, I had an idea. I smiled at Alyssa and said, "Why don't you ride the black horse so you can practice your courage!" After several refusals of my suggestion, one day she agreed. She mounted the horse with me at her side and held on for dear life. When she left the mall that day her joy was overwhelming as she said, "I did it, Meemaw! I practiced my courage!"

Not too long after that victory, we returned to the mall to see the carousel gone. For two or three years after that, she would say, "I wish the black horse was still there so I could practice my courage again." I will always believe that my brave little granddaughter practicing her courage on a carousel horse has helped prepare her for other events to come later in her life which will require courage.

I experienced my own "black horse" when many years ago, I felt lead to apply for the science coordinator position in my school system. I had been a classroom teacher for seventeen years when this opportunity became available, and several people encouraged me to submit an application. I laughed after the first two or three people mentioned it to me, but when others said the same thing I began to ponder if the Lord was sending me a signal. Finally, after yet another person prompted me, I decided to discover if the suggestions were from the Lord. I had never imaged myself having this job and certainly never hoped to achieve this change in my professional life. I was very fearful about even going through the interview process and prayed that I would be offered the position only if it was from God's hand. After I was hired, I literally felt like I had "walked off a cliff with only thin air under my feet."

The months from the end of the school year until the beginning of my moving to this new position were some of the most anxious days of my life. I simply decided to do what I felt what was the Lord's plan for me and practice my own courage in the face of my fear. The Lord drenched me in spiritual blessings and growth during the time I worked in this position, and I will always rejoice that when I "jumped off that cliff", He was there beside me.

I recall many other anxious times when the Lord gave me opportunities to practice my courage to obtain strength. He has been at my side through the illness and death of loved ones, loss of jobs, health crises, and great personal trauma. I also remember the walk of other believers as they also were called on to endure great loss and trials which required supernatural assistance for survival. Courage became a gift, not sought, but valued because it came from the hand of God.

On many occasions in our lives, we experience challenging and uncomfortable situations and the Lord is telling us, "I want you to practice your courage." Certainly, before David approached Goliath in the name of the living God, he had practiced his courage. As a shepherd boy he was called on at times to use his slingshot and rocks to protect his sheep. Many ferocious wild animals would approach and threaten the sheep entrusted to him. As he grew in his role as a protector, he came to know God and trust was woven into the fiber of his being. He knew God was at his side and felt His familiar presence when he stood in front of the giant. He had practiced his courage and his countenance revealed the very character of God.

Moses had the same experiences in the desert with God. He had lived through many stressful times filled with trauma and hardship. God took all of these challenges and transformed them into strength embedded in his soul. Moses drew from this God-given treasure to boldly stand in front of pharaoh, to courageously raise his staff in front of the Red Sea, and to wait confidently on God in the desert to create miracle after miracle.

We have been called to walk with the Lord in our time of challenges and practice our courage in a way that brings Him honor and glory. Remember when your "black horse" comes to submit to a God-given opportunity and let fear take a back seat. Watch for the hand of God to weave a fiber of strength into your being!

Practice your courage under the Lord's guidance and watch fear take a back seat as He strengthens you.

Isaiah 55:8-9

"My thoughts are completely different from yours," says the LORD. "And my ways are far beyond anything you could imagine. For just as the heavens are higher than the earth, so are my ways higher than your ways and my thoughts higher than your thoughts."

CHAPTER EIGHT

God's Unique Prayer Postmarks

$\mathcal{A}$ lan strolled through the woods on a warm, beautiful day on the farm where he had spent many happy years with his grandparents who were no longer living. He was captivated by a huge, warm yellow glow he had never seen before. What could possibly be creating this beautiful vision in such a familiar, but yet unusual setting on his property?

When he arrived at the actual source of the golden light he could scarcely believe his eyes. There on the banks of a stream he had visited during his youth was something he had never before witnessed. His eyes feasted on the sight of huge Chanterelle mushrooms scattered everywhere he looked. He had been asking the Lord for material blessings to cover his unpaid bills that month and God answered this request with mushrooms! He harvested the mushrooms over the next few weeks and sold them to local restaurant owners who were happy to pay him an amount significant to him, but much less than what their regular suppliers charged.

God often has unique ways of answering our heart-rendered prayers, and this is surely only one of millions and millions of His responses matched to believers' needs. I pondered the significance of the mushroom story after Alan's family shared it with me.

I believe it is an example of what the world calls a coincidence, but is actually one of God's inspiring postmarks. I have experienced God answering many of my prayers in unusual and thrilling ways, and I rejoiced that God had provided a magnificent and creative answer to Alan's prayer.

A few days after Alan's discovery, I walked into my back yard and saw several of the same kind of mushrooms resting a few yards from my house. Our home is situated next to a golf course and is in an entirely different setting than the one that provided Alan's mushrooms. My husband and I had lived there for over twenty-five years, and I had never seen them before. I knew the uncommon amount of rain we had experienced during the summer months had brought about conditions favorable for the mushrooms, and the Master Gardner synchronized this observation with Alan's to give me the confirmation that I was seeing one of His postmarks.

God seeks to encourage us in small ways to prepare us for our big battles. I am currently in fervent prayer for another good friend's son-in-law who is being treated for a malignant brain tumor. The tumor had been surgically removed and he had successfully completed radiation and chemotherapy. A follow-up scan a year and a half later revealed an area that gave concern to his doctor, and he asked the insurance company for permission to do another scan focusing on the suspicious area. The doctor believed having this information could be vital to his making decisions about treatment that might save the young man's life. Permission was denied and weeks of prayers were offered as the physician resubmitted his request. Again permission was not given. However, after this second denial, the hospital affiliated with the doctor decided this patient fit the profile they needed for a research project, and he qualified to have the scan done at no charge. Everyone praying for the insurance company to change its decision had not even considered another way God could answer our prayers. God, being who He is, surprised us with another one of His special answers. I believe God gave this young man's family a postmark of encouragement to strengthen them on their faith journey.

There have been times in my life I have been disappointed when God did not seem to answer my prayers for people and situations needing His divine touch. Still, as time has passed and I look over my long life, I see a tapestry of His work that has drenched me in blessings. He has put people in my path to encourage me. He has provided unexpected material and spiritual gifts, and He has provided me with the courage and strength I needed while I waited on Him.

I am thankful for God's character and that His thoughts are not mine. He always has a plan which surpasses what I am able to perceive, and when I go home to be with Him I know I will celebrate what He has done. God's Word says to me that I can trust Him because of who He is. He holds all believers close to His heart, and knowing that gives me knowledge of how valuable I am to Him.

Give your heart's desires and deepest needs to the Lord. Look for God in every aspect of your life, and you will see Him acting on your behalf in ways that the world will never perceive or even notice. Ask Him to shed light on the path He has provided for you. He will amaze you as He directs your steps so you can find the treasure He has stored for you in your days on this earth. No one in the world has the capacity to love and bless us more than Him! Praise Him for who He is! Love Him for who He is and give Him the honor and glory!

Give the Lord every aspect of your life and watch as He acts on your behalf in ways that will surprise the world.

Isaiah 61:10

I am overwhelmed with joy in the LORD my God! For he has dressed me with the clothing of salvation and draped me in a robe of righteousness. I am like a bridegroom for his wedding suit or a bride with her jewels.

CHAPTER NINE

Postmark for the Future: A Beautiful "Premature" Dress

*G*loria had stored the beautiful, long, aqua lace evening gown for two years in the top of a closet. The gorgeous dress had a matching deep aqua satin lining that fell short of the hem of the outer dress by several inches. The contrast in lengths highlighted the lace pattern in the front as the fabric cascaded to the floor. The unworn dress was folded neatly in a box which had been wrapped in rich, gold paper with a huge, shiny silver bow. I had excitedly presented this gift to Gloria a couple of weeks before Christmas. She had then placed it under the Christmas tree that she had lovingly decorated for her mother and family. The dress was given and received in deep abiding love between two friends who had been there for each other for almost forty years.

Gloria and I met when our children were toddlers, and now they are grown with teenagers of their own. Through the years our friendship has strengthened and deepened as we have

walked together through many trials. We have endured tragedy that has captured people we loved, grieved over the death of
family members, fought against life-threatening illnesses, and
shared the anguish of family members suffering through great
misfortune. Our faith walks have been forged with hours of
prayer for each other and with many prayers offered together
with clasped hands. God put us together because He knew we
needed each other, and even though we are not sisters by birth,
we are true sisters in every way that matters the most to our
spirits. We have a great enduring love for each other which
gives us strength and joy.

I bought this gown for Gloria on impulse when I discovered
it on a clearance rack in a quaint store sequestered deep in
the mountains. I have always been an avid shopper and quickly observed it could be purchased for a mere fraction of the
original price. What an incredible bargain! Still, three return
visits were necessary before I could make the final decision. I
knew that my dear friend had been taking care of her adored,
elderly mother for over twelve years, and lately she rarely left
the house for anything but the necessities of daily living. Yet I
yearned to give her a gift that defied that reality. Gloria tried
on the dress, and even though it was found to be an imperfect
fit, it was presented for viewing to her mother and family on
New Year's Eve. After all, it was motivation from a loving heart
that was the real value of the gift. Believing that she would
probably never have an occasion to wear the dress to an actual
event, Gloria sadly placed the dress back in the unwrapped box
and put it in the top of a closet. Periodically, she took the dress
from the closet and wistfully dreamed of wearing it to a special
event in the future.

A year and a half later, Gloria's much-loved mother passed
away, and deeply-felt grief was left in her place. Gloria's husband decided, after almost a year of seeing her carry her heavy
loss, he needed to do something to bring a measure of happiness back into their home. He convinced his wife to go on
a family cruise with two of their granddaughters and a niece
and her children. The trip would be an opportunity for them
to spend a week together on a ship dedicated to fun and relax-
ation.

Gloria began to nervously consider the clothing choices

and purchases needed to prepare for such a trip. She had never before experienced anything like this vacation and really was not certain where to begin. She suddenly remembered the box in the top of the closet. Perhaps with some alterations, the formal would meet the needs of the evening attire required for the cruise. She carefully removed the dress from the tissue in the box and slipped it over her head and felt it slide easily over her hips. She could not believe the image of herself in the mirror! It now fit perfectly and looked like it had been made for her and purchased just for the Caribbean adventure that awaited her.

The aqua lace gown was a huge hit on the cruise ship! Gloria could hardly make her way forward to the dining area, without one person after another stopping her to tell her how breathtaking she looked. At least twenty times, she stopped to hear adoring comments from total strangers. For many years, she had worn clothes appropriate for her job as a beautician, and then for thirteen years she had dressed to be a caregiver for her mother. Dressing up was a very rare event, and being adored and admired for her appearance in an exclusive dress made her feel like royalty!

God knew that the dress purchased with an imperfect fit and with no apparent opportunity for wearing would be a postmark for Gloria to savor for the future. God was in that dress shop whispering to me so I could be a part of His story of hope and comfort for a beloved daughter who had unselfishly cared for her mother. It was purchased as a symbol of promise for the future.

I believe that some day when I go to my real home in heaven, I, as well as all believers, will be dressed in the righteousness of God. All of us who call Him Father will be adorned with garments that glow and glisten in the presence of His light. Super colossal joy awaits us there as packages under Christmas trees symbolize here on Earth! Hope dwells in our spirits as we perceive what is scheduled for our future and already exists in the perception of eternity that God places in our hearts.

Do you have an unused source of treasure from God that you have received and hidden away because you do not feel a need or an occasion for its use? Do you know what that gift means for people living in today's stressful times? It is the Word of God waiting for you to retrieve it so you can discover its perfect fit for your mind, spirit, and body. Find a Bible that you have purchased somewhere in days past and begin reading and savoring the miracle of God-given words of hope and salvation. Make this experience a daily conversation with the living God! Praise Him! Praise Him!

Daily discover the treasure of God's Word in your Bible. It is a perfect fit for your life.

Psalm 34:18

The LORD is close to the brokenhearted. He rescues those whose spirits are crushed.

Psalm 147:3

He heals the brokenhearted and bandages their wounds.

Psalm 51:17

The sacrifice you desire is a broken spirit. You will not reject a broken and repentant heart, O God.

Isaiah 57:15

The high and lofty one who lives in eternity, the Holy One, says this: "I live in the high and holy place with those whose spirits are contrite and humble. I restore the crushed spirit of the humble and revive the courage of those with repentant hearts."

CHAPTER TEN

God's Comforting Postmark: Broken Things Restored

*M*y ninety-one-year old mother carefully lifted the broken bowl from the packing material of the cardboard box it had arrived in a few days earlier. When this piece of china had been purchased about one hundred years previously, it had been very expensive. It was decorated with beautiful hand-painted flowers highlighted with touches of real gold. Unfortunately this antique bowl now had a huge crack that went from one side to the other. The large amount of glue used to repair the bowl over fifty years ago had yellowed with age.

Mother sadly told me why she was now in possession of this bowl. She said, "Your sister has kept this for me for many years, but she and her husband are in the process of moving to a much smaller home, and they have sold the china closet where it was stored. Since they no longer have a place for the bowl, they thought I might like to have it back."

At the time Mother was living in a small apartment, and she also had no space for it. However, she asked my sister to mail it to her. The appraised value of the bowl, had it been in perfect condition, would have been a few hundred dollars. Mother could not bear to dispose of the dish because it had belonged to a favorite aunt, and it had immeasurable sentimental value for her.

She told me the story of her aunt moving many years ago from her home to smaller quarters and giving her this treasured piece of china. She chose Mother because she believed she was the one family member who would value it and take care of it.

Mother at the time was young, and she and my father were struggling to make ends meet. They had used inexpensive second-hand furniture to decorate their home which did not include a cabinet that could house an expensive piece of china.

Mother had placed the bowl in the top of a closet and put blankets around it to protect it. Much later, forgetting what was housed in the blankets, she reached into the closet to retrieve one of the them. The dish tumbled out and broke into two pieces. Tearfully, she hurried to find some glue and lavishly put it on the dish to cement the pieces back together. My mother's aunt was correct when she gave it to her knowing she would greatly value this bowl, but Mother was devastated she had let her aunt down by accidentally breaking it.

Mother also shared with me why her aunt had been so special to her. She told the story of how her Aunt Ada had been a faithful member of a Methodist Church and had decided the Lord had called her to be a pastor and share His Word with the world. At that time, women in the Methodist Church were not allowed to be pastors. So she sadly left the church and became a pastor in a Nazarene Church. I was very moved that my great aunt, who had long left this world, was such a voice of faith. When Mother asked me, "Do you have any place for this bowl in your home?" I saw a door of opportunity to see another of God's postmarks.

My first instinct was to resist putting a cracked piece of china in my overwhelmed home of "stuff." Indeed my husband said every time I took a trip to the thrift store with several boxes of "treasures" from our cluttered closets, "Well, there goes another teaspoon out of the ocean!" However, I surprised myself by saying, "I know exactly where it belongs." The Holy Spirit had whispered into my thoughts that this beautiful broken bowl was meant for me and it belonged in the prayer room of my home.

Later, Mother's information about her aunt reluctantly leaving her church to answer a call to the ministry resonated in my mind. I remembered when the first female pastor of our church was announced, I was disappointed. I was prepared to be unsupportive of her until I clearly heard these words in my spirit, "But what if I have called you to be an advocate for her?" In that moment, I knew the Lord had spoken to me. I instantly had a love for her, even though I had never met her. Now, I had a postmark from the Lord revealing to me why He had chosen me to be an advocate for our church's first female pastor.

I could not contain my joy in realizing this beautiful bowl would not have come to me if it had not been broken. The value the world would have placed on it would have resulted in it being somewhere else. I knew the Lord had done this just for me! Just as He keeps track of our tears (Psalm 56:8) He was keeping a record of whose hands touched this dish.

I have always been attracted to damaged objects and will occasionally purchase them on the discount shelves of stores to take them home and attempt to restore them. A few years ago, I accidentally broke a large vase that was sitting on the floor of a store. I went to the store owner and told her what I had done and offered to pay for it. She was very kind and said "That's all right. I appreciate your honesty and I will not charge you." I told her I really did need to pay for the vase. I knew that my integrity for the Lord was at stake. I was enormously grateful when I was told that its cost was around $15.00. I was afraid my honesty was going to come with a much higher price tag! Later, the Lord blessed that transaction in an unexpected way. The store owner and I became good friends. One day, after store hours, I prayed with her for the Lord's blessing on her business. The Lord gave us evidence of His favor with comments that some of her customers made. They would remark, "There is something special about the atmosphere of this store!"

Surprisingly the vase I took home the day I met this store owner took on unexpected value. I used my hot glue gun to put the pieces back together. I also glued various small flowers and leaves over the exposed, cracked places. I found some large silk flowers in one of my closets and placed them in the vase. I was surprised to see how beautiful the vase had become! In this moment I clearly heard a message from the Lord: "That was you in your brokenness and now that I have restored you, your beauty is before me. This is how I see you."

Remembering this experience, I was inspired to see what could be done with mother's antique bowl. I removed all the excess yellow glue and attached a small gold branch with tiny leaves from the local craft store across the crack. It was no longer obvious it had been damaged. When I showed it to Mother, she was stunned at the restoration!

This postmark from the Lord taught me a lesson I will never forget. If my Great Aunt Ada's antique bowl had been in perfect condition, it would not have come to me. If I had never suffered a shattered spirit, I would have never come to the Lord. I would have never experienced the healing, peace and comfort that has come to me from the hand of the living God. I would have never been made new in my spirit and possessed the joy of being rescued from my plight. I would not have the testimony He bestowed upon me.

King David gave testimony to the saving grace of the Lord as he wrote many of the Psalms. When he wrote about God being near and extending His hand to save those who were crushed in spirit, healing their spirits, and even binding up their wounds, he was speaking from personal experiences.

Are you experiencing any brokenness in your life? Although painful to our spirits, it is the pain of this experience that molds our character closer to the character of God than anything else. The Lord is reaching out to you to bring restoration, peace, and wholeness to your life. He is near to you and is extending His hand to save you who are crushed in spirit. He heals the broken-hearted and binds up their wounds. Come! Our God is waiting for you. Praise Him for He is our Mighty Healer!

Let God heal your broken-heartedness and heal your wounds.

Luke 9:23

Then he said to them all: "If anyone would come after me, he must deny himself and take up his cross daily and follow me. For whoever wants to save his life will lose it, but whoever loses his life for me will save it."

Haggai 2:18-19:

"On this eighteenth day of December—the day when the foundation of the LORD"s temple was laid—carefully consider this: I am giving you a promise now while the seed is still in the barn, before you have harvested your grain and before the grapevine, the fig tree, the pomegranate, and the olive tree have produced their crops. From this day onward I will bless you."

CHAPTER ELEVEN

Postmark for All Believers: The Shadow of the Cross

*T*he shadow of a large cross loomed on the bedroom wall the morning of the wedding. The young, soon-to-be groom, awoke to find the image facing him as he arose from his bed. His last night as a single man had seemed very long. He had been restless and unable to relax and sleep. Images of white crosses placed along highways to commemorate where automobile accident victims had lost their lives flashed through his mind. Making the connection between those crosses and what he saw on his wall made him laugh nervously. He hoped the image on his wall was not a sign of the future, foreshadowing what he might experience in his marriage.

He had dated his fiancé for three years, and they had been very much in love since the first few months. Eight months earlier they had decided on a wedding date to correspond with the completion of her education at a university located one hundred miles from his college. Together they had counted off the days until their wedding. She was going to finish her student-teaching at a location near their new home, and then hopefully secure a teaching position to finance his last year in veterinary school.

At the time of this writing the young man in this story and his wife recently celebrated forty-eight years of marriage. The image of the cross has been so memorable for the husband that for almost forty years he has loved retelling the story about the morning of their wedding. He always laughed about what the Lord might have been telling him about the future with his wife-to-be. For him it was a humorous story, and he had a lot of fun telling it over and over.

However, his interpretation of the now long ago event changed when, at the age of sixty, he attended a three-day Christian retreat. When he returned home, he made a first time commitment to the Lord. His wife tearfully stood by him as he was baptized and joined the church he had attended sporadically for the past thirty years. He lovingly told her, "Your prayers during all the past years kept me close to the Lord. I now know the true significance of the shadow of the cross I saw all those years ago. The Lord was telling me, He would bless our marriage."

What a wondrous revelation it was for me to hear those words when my husband shared them with me a few years ago. Yes, the young man in this story is my beloved husband of all these years—Larry! The shadow of the cross was an amazing postmark from the Lord.

Much later I came across some Scripture I had not noticed before. The prophet Haggai from the Old Testament is frequently overlooked because this book consists of only two chapters and is infrequently quoted. Haggai lived when the Israelites had returned from captivity in Babylon to their homeland and were rebuilding the temple. I was stunned to see Haggai 2:18-19: "On this eighteenth day of December- the day when the foundation of the LORD's temple was laid-carefully consider this: I am giving you a promise now while the seed is still in the barn, before you have harvested your grain and before the grapevine, the fig tree, the pomegranate, and the olive tree have produced their crops. From this day onward I will bless you." Larry and I were married on December 18, 1965. On our wedding day the foundation for a Christian marriage had been laid, and God had given a sign of this promise.

This story received another chapter long after the first one had been written. When Larry was in college, he had been part of a trio that sang at various locations on campus, but after graduation the trio disbanded and the three went in different directions. Larry stopped singing for almost forty years. I yearned to hear his beautiful voice again. Whenever we stood together during the congregation hymns in our church service, I would strain to hear that marvelous voice I remembered from all those years ago.

After my husband joined our church, I pleaded with a friend who was in the choir, "Please ask Larry to join the choir. He loved to sing many years ago, and I know he would truly be blessed by participating in the choir." Later she told me that she had extended the invitation and he had told her "No." Not giving up that easily, I told her that we needed to "pray" him into the choir. Still he kept saying "No." Then one day he said "Yes. I will give it a try." I believe with all my heart that the Lord answered that prayer for His honor and glory!

When Larry first joined the choir, participating in the process of learning music that blended so many other voices in beautiful, harmonious songs was a huge challenge for him. He sadly told me, "After all this time, my voice is gone, and I just can't sing anymore. It is just too late!"

Time and again the Lord loves to work in situations just like this one to surprise us. Larry decided to buy a karaoke machine to practice his music. Then the Lord did something unexpected by anointing this piece of equipment to bless his voice. After two years, Larry's voice came back with a new found confidence, and he began to sing solos in public for the first time in his life. He developed a ministry of music that took him to funerals, social functions for senior citizen groups, adult day care centers, and Christian conferences.

Every time I see the Lord's hand on my husband's life as He uses him as a vessel to bless so many people in our community, I am absolutely thrilled! When we were dating he would occasionally send me a tape of his music, and I know hearing his wonderful voice helped me to fall deeply in love with him. Today, when I hear him sing, I become young again and fall even more in love with him. That's a miraculous gift from the Lord for a couple of lovebirds in their late sixties.

Hearing my husband sing in the choir during worship services at our church has been one of the greatest blessings of my life. I frequently tell Larry, "I know when you sing in the choir, the angels are there singing and rejoicing with you and the others." He occasionally gives me a skeptical look and sometimes laughs when he responds, "Well where were those angels today? We struggled on that song."

On one particular Sunday I asked the Lord to confirm my belief that His angels were indeed participating in our worship services. Halfway through the choir's anthem, I saw a shadow on my husband's forehead. I could not determine what had created the image until he sat down after the choir had finished their song. It was then that I looked up at the large gold cross that hangs suspended from the cathedral ceiling of our church sanctuary. That same shadow appeared on the wall behind the cross. It was made by the lower portion of the cross. During the thirty years that I had been in the church I had never seen that particular sight. The following Sunday another choir member stood in exactly the same place where Larry had been, and there was no shadow of the cross on his forehead. I believe my prayer, my spirit, and physical circumstances were synchronized by the Holy Spirit in a "God-given" moment to give me a testimony to share with others.

I feel assured the Lord answered my prayer so I could see with my eyes what my heart had revealed to me. His blessing was there on my husband's voice and the voices of all the other worshippers in the service. God is always there among us when we worship and praise Him, and His angels are there rejoicing with us.

The cross is a postmark for all believers. If you envisioned an invisible imprint of the cross in your spirit, what difference would that make on your decisions, attitudes, actions and everything you do? Certainly, Satan sees evidence of this invisible mark in us, and he strives to motivate us to exhibit behavior that makes this sign a lie for our lives. Monitor those things that feed your mind such as movies, television, reading material, technology resources, and music. Stay grounded in the Word of God to saturate every pathway in your daily living so others may know the victory that awaits all of us in the shadow of the cross!

Envision an invisible cross in your spirit when you make decisions about what goes into your mind and spirit.

Isaiah 45:2-3

This is what the LORD says: "I will go before you, Cyrus, and level the mountains. I will smash down gates of bronze and cut through bars of iron. And I will give you treasures hidden in the darkness—secret riches. I will do this so you may know that I am the LORD, the God of Israel, the one who calls you by name."

CHAPTER TWELVE

Postmarks in Precious Things Lost

*I*n the midst of people who were visiting with each other after our church service, my good friend, Linda, and I stood in the narthex of our church and prayed. She recently had lost an expensive piece of jewelry during a shopping trip in a town several miles from her home. We stood there in faith believing that God cares about all matters in our lives whether they are considered by us to be of large or small importance.

Many years ago, when my husband and I lived in another state, I had a fantastic Christian friend who encouraged me to pray about everything. She always said, "If you only consult with the Lord on the really big things in your life, you will not be talking to Him on a regular basis!" Believing God cares about even the small details of my life has encouraged me through the years to pray for things I have misplaced. On the occasions when the Lord gave His divine assistance with the search, He always wrapped that discovery in a message of faith.

Being blessed by the Lord in this way has inspired me to encourage others to pray for any lost item which has importance to them, and I frequently join them in prayer. I can testify that often the Lord reveals the location of a lost item along with a powerful spiritual message. After all, our Lord is the master of the "lost and found."

Linda has always possessed a radiant smile and "lights up any room" she enters. Recently she worked diligently to lose a significant amount of weight, and although she was delighted to wear smaller clothing, she also discovered that some of her favorite jewelry was now too large. She impulsively decided to wear a multi-diamond ring, which had great sentimental value, on a shopping excursion, believing that even though it was loose on her finger, it would stay in place. When she returned home, to her great dismay, she discovered her beautiful ring was missing. She frantically called all the stores where she had shopped and was told that no one had found the ring. With a heavy heart, she left her name and telephone number with each person she spoke to.

It had been several days since she lost her ring when we stood in prayer in our church. She reminded me she lost a bracelet two years ago and that we had prayed about that with no results. Undeterred, I said "We will just pray and see what the Lord has in His plans for your ring!"

A week later, before we began our ladies' Bible study my friend excitedly shared with me some terrific news. "A store just called to tell me they found my ring! It had fallen under a chest of drawers." Evidently this piece of furniture had been in the store for quite some time and had recently sold soon after our prayer. The ring was discovered when the chest was moved. Even though the band of the ring had been damaged, the diamonds were in great condition.

A couple of weeks afterwards my friend proudly wore the refurbished ring to our Bible study. She excitedly told the ladies how her answered prayer had blessed her. We all praised the Lord for this answered prayer, knowing that had the ring been lost forever, we would have still stood and given Him praise for who He is and His love for us. We had asked the Lord to use this lost ring for His honor and glory, and we joyfully realized He was giving us an opportunity to be participants in His answer.

Recently in our church we experienced a dramatic reminder that God hears our prayers when much has been lost. A couple, who had been long-time members, lost their home, car, and all their personal belongings in a devastating fire while they were out of the country. After receiving the news a few days before their scheduled return, they sent an email to our pastor which he read the following Sunday to the entire congregation. At the time they were traveling in a very poor country where the population existed with few resources. Their message revealed how blessed they felt even though they had lost all their possessions. With hearts of faith they said, "We weigh our loss in the midst of people with a very meager existence and realize how fortunate we are to have so much. We look forward to returning and rebuilding our home." Many tears were shed when we heard their message of hope in the midst of great loss.

After returning home they spent long hours sifting through the debris to see if they could uncover anything of value in the ashes that had once been their home. Two treasures were found which no amount of insurance could replace. One of them was the china her father had given them many years ago when her mother died. Her father was a Methodist minister and had purchased the set at a church meeting in Japan several years ago. Over the years the china had been lovingly packed by her mother for each move as her family went from parsonage to parsonage. The china was a small piece of home accompanying the family to each new location. Having the set in their own home all these years later represented a continuance of the love that had touched them over the years.

Also discovered in the rubble was a diamond tie-tack the husband had been given at the time of his father's death. The diamond was from his grandmother's wedding ring and had been greatly treasured by his father. Finding something that small and yet so valued was remarkable.

I believe that my friends were touched by the hand of God to give them a postmark of His presence in the "home" of their hope and faith. So many fervent prayers had been lifted on their behalf by all of us in the church for them to have comfort, and even joy, in the midst of their plight. We could feel the power of our living God as it swept through our spirits, and we began to receive revelation through our friends' loss. Hearing their testimony, as they praised God while experiencing the restoration of their material lives, brought much honor and glory to our Father.

Isaiah 45:2-3 gives prophecy about how the Lord provides treasures in secret and dark places. Sometimes, I believe the treasures are under a chest of drawers waiting to be sold, or in the ashes of a home completely destroyed by fire. Sometimes they are deep in the hearts of God's children who wait to be healed.

What have you lost in your life that has brought you to a point of hopelessness? What lies in the hidden places of your heart that cries out for healing? Pray for the Lord to level the mountains in your life and smash down the gates of bronze and bars of iron that prevent you from receiving the treasures He has waiting for you. He will do this so that you may know that it is He, the God of Israel, who calls you by name!

Let God heal the hidden places of your heart that cry out in pain.

Romans 8:28

And we know that God causes everything to work together for the good of those who love God and are called according to His purpose for them.

CHAPTER THIRTEEN
God's Surprising Postmarks with Collages

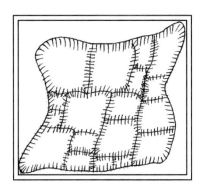

I peered closely at the collage of striking colors: red, hot-pink, light-pink, lime-green, tangerine, and yellow which were embedded in the fleece squares sewn together to make an eye-catching throw. The lime-green squares were accented with a ladybugs and daisies print. The rectangular sides were fringed giving a beautiful texture to the throw. These vibrant colors matched those I had used in a bedroom in our home. Even the ladybug print was complementary to the one in the custom made valences and bed skirts in this bedroom. My granddaughters frequently spent the night in this room and referred to it as the "girls' bedroom."

This unusual throw had been displayed in the midst of other hand-made items in a fabric store in Washington, Indiana known as the "Stitching Post." This store is owned by one of my favorite cousins, Mary Dell, who I also refer to as my "sister." Mary Dell revealed to me the history of the creation of this fabric collage. It seems all the pieces had been scraps from several bolts of fleece, and Mary Dell had sent them home with an employee and challenged her to see what her creativity might do with them. This beautiful project of leftover pieces was the result of that assignment. Every piece appeared to have been part of a well thought-out design and no one could have surmised by the appearance that it was an inspired afterthought!

After I issued many admiring comments and several "bold hints" Mary Dell gave the throw to me. I happily took my treasure back home to Georgia and spread it across one of the beds in the "girls" bedroom. In the midst of all the complementary pieces, the throw looked like it had been made especially for the room.

Appreciating the way the beautiful throw completed the total look of a room frequently filled with the love and laughter of my granddaughters inspired me to ponder a different kind of a collage—that of some of my life experiences. I have been through several periods of time which were dominated by failure and sadness with no perceivable satisfaction or reward of any kind. I classified them as "scraps" meriting forgetfulness to protect my feelings of self-worth and ward off any loss of joy. One of these "scraps" happened when I was only fourteen, and one of my mother's casual friends called her and asked if I would be interested in working a few hours a week in her restaurant. A work permit would be necessary, and this job would result in a few long days for me during the school year. However, I was thrilled at the prospect of earning some spending money.

After being employed for only one month, I was released because I simply didn't seem to have the skills required for being an effective waitress. I was hired because my mother's friend believed my outstanding grades as a student would match what she needed for her employees. I cried bitterly the night that I was let go, and my mother was indignant that anyone would fire her daughter!

It was many years later, after I graduated as the valedictorian of my high school class and entered Indiana University, I realized God's hand was at work in this embarrassing time. He was saving me from a situation that was not a part of His long-term plan for me. The few weeks I worked impacted the time I had available to study, and I was constantly tired from being a working student. Graduating at the top of my high school class provided a small scholarship for my studies to be a teacher and would have been forfeited had I continued to work. I simply could not continue to earn exceptional grades and maintain a job in a restaurant. God stretched out His hand to allow me a failure and give me tremendous success in another area of my life. This "scrap" became a piece of the tapestry of my faith.

Throughout my teaching career I interviewed for many positions as I moved with my husband and family. Frequently I received no hope or encouragement as I submitted my applications, but the refusals were simply God's protection on me as He guided me to the classrooms He had selected for me. His constant provision "fringed" these scraps of negativity into the texture of my faith walk.

At one point in my career in education I was in a science leadership position for four years, but due to a huge financial challenge within the school system, I was released along with others who had the same positions in other academic areas. A few years after returning to the classroom I received a national teaching award, The Presidential Award for Science Teaching, which included a week-long trip to Washington D.C. The whole experience was thrilling for me and my husband who accompanied me on this trip. Had I remained in an administrative leadership position, I would not have been in place in my classroom to have this experience of a lifetime!

Time after time in my life, I have seen the living God weave experiences that felt like failures into a beautiful garment of faith for me to wear. Just like the cutting of the fabric provided fringes on the beautiful throw given to me by my cousin, the experiences that "cut" into my feelings of self-worth were carefully woven to provide strength, trust, courage, and humility in my spirit. Looking back over my long life, I have come to believe that God's hand has always been on me, and He has left nothing to chance.

God's Word reveals many thrilling examples of His weaving together the tapestry of believers' lives in ways that have blessed many generations throughout the ages. The Old Testament gives us many stories which teach these lessons of faith. Joseph suffered the enormous hurt and humiliation of being thrown into a pit by his own brothers, and later into prison based on the lies of pharaoh's wife, only later to be in position to become a dynamic leader in Egypt. God used Joseph to save

His people and give testimony for all the ages.

David, a man after God's own heart, spent many years after he was anointed to be the next King of Israel in caves trying to escape Saul's attempts to kill him. God used this stressful time of crushing turmoil to mold David into the King and leader he would become. Some of the Psalms written by David during this part of his life provide hope and encouragement to millions of believers living today. This Scripture could not have possibly been written without the flow of adversity in David's spirit. David's words reveal the presence of the living God walking with him, protecting him, and preserving the lineage that would bring forth our Savior Jesus Christ into a hurting world.

The living God always has a greater plan for the lives of His children than they could possibly perceive. All the days of God's people are used by Him to create living masterpieces of faith walks to call forth His kingdom. We will see what He has done with the texture of our lives when we walk into our eternal home to be bathed by His light and glory.

Trust God with those times in your life that bring personal turmoil and great despair. He will bring beauty and riches to the "collage" of your faith walk which will bless you and many around you.

You may not know some of those being blessed, and some may well realize that blessing in future years. The living God knows how to use our lives to weave together experiences which birth miracles in our lives and in the lives of others! Praise Him for who He is!

God can weave together your life experiences to birth miracles for you and others.

Psalm 104:33

I will sing to the LORD as long as I live. I will praise my God to my last breath!

Zephaniah 3: 16-17

"Cheer up, Zion! Don't be afraid! For the LORD your God has arrived to live among you. He is a mighty savior. He will rejoice over you with great gladness. With his love, he will calm all your fears. He will exult over you by singing a happy song."

CHAPTER FOURTEEN

God's Postmark in a Choir: The Shepherd's Voice Resonates in the Midst of a Church Choir

*M*y surprised friends who sat in the front pews almost fell out of their seats laughing when they saw me that first Sunday sitting in the front row of the choir loft in our church. For many years I had joked about my lack of ability to sing. I had decided that lowering expectations was one way to avoid surprising people with my lack of singing proficiency!

Actually, I had sung in a choir and even performed solos for my hometown church when I was young. As a teenager I had even briefly taken voice lessons, but quite honestly, the standards for evaluating singing ability in my circumstances were very, very low. At that time, volunteering my talent put me at the top of the list for opportunities to sing, and since I could actually "carry a tune," I was really special at this very small church.

My husband, Larry, had been a member of our church's choir for only a few years, but his time in the choir seemed to have greatly enhanced his worship experience. He would return from choir practice many nights telling me about the inspired direction of our choir leader. Worship was obviously being experienced, even when the choir members struggled to learn new songs which challenged their comfort zones, strived to remember the prescribed dynamics for the written music, and blend and synchronize their voices of different ability levels.

I was absolutely thrilled to see Larry stand and sing in the choir during church services. His face radiated joy when he sang, and once I even saw the shadow of a cross above his head as he sung. Realizing his music ministry was born from his experiences in the choir reminded me that the Lord is present every Sabbath day accomplishing unseen miracles in the spirits of believers.

At times I can hear the choir's music resonate throughout the sanctuary as if hundreds of voices are present. I believe when Christians raise their voices praising the Lord they are joined by hundreds of unseen angels. At times, I can even feel the presence of those angels. I sometimes share this belief with my husband, and on occassion, he says, "Where were the angels today? We didn't perform very well on the anthem!" I then respond, "I wish you could have heard what I heard. Be assured, the Lord was glorified today by the music!"

Even though I have an average voice and struggled to sing the hymns during church services, my husband encouraged me to join him in the choir. Quite frankly, I considered his suggestion to be ridiculous! I had been sitting in the congregation with family members and listening to the choir for over thirty years, and that was the way I was comfortable worshipping on Sunday mornings. Some of our family members left over the years to join other churches, but my ninety-three-old mother and I were still a pretty good team in a pew near the front of the church.

When my sister and her husband, who live a few hundred miles away, retired recently, they invited Mother to come and live with them. Unlike my husband and me, they did not have adult children and grandchildren nearby. They believed they could provide a secure and happy situation for Mother. Understanding this might be a good decision for Mother, and actually being happy about her leaving were two different challenging ideas for me to grasp. The first few Sundays after Mother left, I frequently shed tears during the church service as I sat alone. I had been totally spoiled in the thirty-five years I had attended my church in being blessed by always having a family member sit next to me.

Larry reminded me that I could most likely eliminate my problem of loneliness by joining him in the choir. Honestly, my heart was all for it, but my head was saying "Are you crazy?" Finally, when I tried to encourage another friend, who has a lovely voice to join the choir, I told her, "I will join if you will also come!" We made our agreement and I fearfully wondered about what I had done. When I called Mother to share this decision with her, she told me, "I am proud of you!" Upon hearing her words I thought, "She's remembering my voice as it sounded when I was a teenager, and her memory of me singing most assuredly has been embellished over the past fifty years!" I could only pray that the angels would not stop singing with the choir!

I have always known the choir loft is an anointed place in our church. Many times I pray for the Lord to synchronize choir members' voices in a way that will bring Him honor and glory. Once before the choir stood to sing, I literally felt vibrations go through my feet, but I could not identify a source for this strange sensation. My husband said he had not felt anything like what I described. I knew the Lord was giving me a postmark to confirm that He was there.

On another occasion when the choir performed an Easter cantata for two worship services, Larry and I shared with each other that we felt a tingling, vibrating sensation over our entire bodies after each performance. Before the services began, a man, who was one of four people accompanying the choir on musical instruments, shared that he was with us because he had experienced a miracle. He had been in a devastating car accident three years earlier, and while his life was in the balance, the prayers of our church had lifted him up. God had placed him alongside the choir as a sign that He was anointing our message to the congregation about the life, death, and resurrection of Jesus Christ.

I practice our choir songs on a keyboard my husband and I purchased, listen to CD's provided by our choir director, and locate internet sites and YouTube videos of the selected choir music. My worship time with the Lord has increased ten-fold over what I experienced sitting in the church pew with the congregation!

Participating in the choir has bestowed upon me a wealth of blessings that are woven into in the tapestry of my faith. During practice sessions I see the Lord's hand on our spirit-filled director, I see the love among choir members as they share about illnesses and concerns of theirs and family members, I drink in the laughter from those who are drenched in joy, and I leave every evening of practice touched by God's grace and full of His Spirit.

Sunday mornings before our choir members take their places in the choir loft, a prayer is offered asking the Lord to touch the music in a way that will bring Him honor and glory. Some Sundays the music and voices ring out beautifully and spectacularly in ways that causes the congregation to clap and say, "Amen." On other days of worship, the music comes in quiet, hushed tones that cause people to silently reflect as they sit in their pews. No outward sign of acceptance is offered, but God's spirit has been poured out on them. All music that comes from the choir is sung joyously and reverently as an offering to the Lord. The value of this offering is measured in the heart of each person who comes and sits in this anointed place.

Wherever you place your feet, wherever you sit, wherever you speak, wherever you sing for the glory of the Lord, He will not allow it to return back to Himself without great value. He will surround you with His angels to insure that you are mighty for the sake of His kingdom's work. Praise Him with your voice this day. Praise the living God!!!!!

Praise God with your voice today wherever you place your feet.

2 Corinthians 4:18

So we don't look at the troubles we can see right now; rather, we look forward to what we have not yet seen. For the troubles we see will soon be over, but the joys to come will last forever.

Hebrews 11:3

By faith we understand that the entire universe was formed at God's command, that what we now see did not come from anything that can be seen.

CHAPTER FIFTEEN
Postmarks Invisible to the Naked Eye

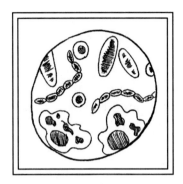

*M*y students peered over their microscopes looking at prepared slides of onion cells, blood cells, and chloroplast found inside green plants. They were seeing some of God's marvelous postmarks—images of objects that can only be seen with the magnification of a microscope. I can remember when I was a student and I pricked my finger so I could see my blood through the lens of a microscope. The blood cells seemed to dance around. My teacher explained that this was the result of random movement caused by subtle vibration. This practical explanation did not diminish my excitement. I was thrilled to see such activity in a drop of blood that had been a part of me. Looking through a microscope was like looking into another world.

Every time I looked at specimens under a microscope I felt that I was given a revelation about some of the awesome things that God does in this world that usually go unnoticed. So much of the time we base our beliefs only on what we can see, and even then we miss many spectacular sights in our environment. I know I have missed seeing too many sunrises and sunsets that were gigantic masterpieces created by my Father because my focus was on things of little value.

All during the thirty-seven years I spent as a science teacher I was driven by the motivation that my students' classroom experiences had the potential to reveal to them the beauty the living God had placed in the world. Aware of the legal obstacles placed in the path of Christian teachers, I nevertheless tried to become a vessel for the presence of the Lord in my classroom. I believe that nothing can keep Him out of any location where a believer places his feet. He resides inside every teacher who knows Him by name, and His imprint is on every lesson taught inside a classroom dedicated to Him.

I recall an instance when I set up a lab for my middle school students so they could examine goldfish tails wrapped in wet gauze under a microscope. After showing the class how to be protective in handling the fish, I set my students loose so they could observe the blood cells moving through the blood vessels in the fishes' tails. The excitement in the room was amazing and was worth the trip I made to the pet store! My silent message to them was, "Look closely inside God's world and be intrigued."

Many thrilling things are happening every day that we are unable to see. Molecules in all kinds of gases and liquids are in constant movement. Even the molecules in solid objects are not perfectly still. Scientists say they "jiggle". Everything is made of smaller particles called atoms and inside atoms there are subatomic particles in constant motion. Everything in this world created by the living God is moving! God created a world that is never still, but instead is resonating from the energy delivered through His design.

One of the last lessons I taught in the classroom was a microscope lab for elementary students. I told them the story of the early inventor of the microscope, Anton Van Leeuwenhoek, who lived in the 1600's. He was a shopkeeper who experimented with lenses and developed a tool to look at bacteria, yeast cells, water drops thriving with organism activity, and various blood cells. His findings were absolutely stunning for the time in which he lived. He suffered much verbal abuse from people around him who could not see what he was observing and thought he should devote his time to more productive work. I tried to help my students simulate some of his early activities with hand lenses so they could use their imagination to "walk back" into his era.

The most important knowledge from the lessons on microscopes and lenses was the significance of this invention. Progress in medicine and technology in the last few hundred years is riveted around the advances some courageous scientists such as Van Leeuwenhoek brought forth into this world. Surely these inventions were inspired by God to reveal some of His master design.

My greatest learning objective for my students was for them to realize that each of them has God-given potential that might not be recognized by people around them. Those around Van Leeuwenhoek failed to see how his discovery could impact on the well-being of millions of people throughout the ages, but yet his inspiration led him to continue. Discovering the touch of the Creator on this world, and realizing one's role to share this discovery with others, are to experience being fully alive for the glory of God.

God has surrounded us with evidence of His majesty and might. What is often unseen in the world sometimes reveals God's most thrilling and amazing postmarks. Seek God every day of your life and capture for your remembrance those thrilling moments when you feel His presence. Put on your "spiritual lenses" and watch life pulsating through the universe that was born from the hand of the living God. Realize the potential He has placed inside you and become a part of this life force for His honor and glory!

Seek God every day of your life and capture those thrilling moments when you feel His presence.

Psalm 56:8

You keep track of all of my sorrows. You have collected all my tears in your bottle. You have recorded each one in your book.

Revelation 5:8

And as he took the scroll, the four living beings and the twenty-four elders fell down before the Lamb. Each one had a harp, and they held gold bowls filled with incense—the prayers of God's people.

CHAPTER SIXTEEN

Sentimental Postmarks That Let Us Know We Are Valued

*M*y husband, Larry, handed me a fifty-year-old memory in the form of a small piece of paper with a handwritten address. Somehow he had managed to save it for over half a century and the address was written by me on the very first day we met. At that time, I was a freshman at Indiana University in Bloomington, Indiana and had traveled to Purdue University in West Lafayette, Indiana to visit my cousin, Mary Dell. When Mary Dell's Cooperative House at Purdue desperately needed a substitute bowler for a league bowling match, I reluctantly allowed myself to be "drafted". Larry bowled on the opposing team, and I like to believe that he was "bowled over" when we met that day! He called me later that afternoon for a date where we exchanged addresses with the expectation that we would write to each other.

Our universities were over one hundred miles apart, so we were able to see each other only every two or three weeks. The letters he sent were very important to me. We met during a period of time that had not yet seen e-mail, texting, cell phones, iPads, streaming, Skyping, etc. I could not wait to receive his letters, and it simply did not occur to me that once the letters began to go back and forth he would have any reason to save the slip of paper with my original address written on it.

Throughout our long marriage we have had times where we were unhappy with each other, and there certainly have been a few arguments over the years. One of our differences was that I was sentimental and liked romantic gestures, and Larry did not seem to be of that mind. In one of our first years of marriage I spent a few hours on Valentine's Day making my husband a large decorated heart-shaped cookie. I happily presented it to him and was immediately crushed with his total lack of enthusiasm. I ended up eating the cookie myself because he didn't want it! There have also been a few forgotten birthdays and uninspired or absent gifts on other special occasions.

Larry had made me feel like a "million dollars" when we dated for three years, and I thought this kind of effort would extend throughout our lifetime together. I suffered from a common female mind-set about how my "knight in shining armor" should behave to make me feel adored! That was a lot of responsibility and expectation for my young husband.

It's interesting how husbands and wives transform during a long, committed marriage. In the last several years Larry has become more romantic and sentimental, and I have become less intense about these things. I remember all the times I suffered not too quietly with hurt feelings, and he put up with me. I guess he thought I was worth the trouble. He once told me it wasn't that he didn't want to give me fantastic, thoughtful presents—it was just that he was looking for the "perfect" present and couldn't figure out what it was.

During all our years of our marriage, he had secretly saved a slip of paper commemorating our first exchange because it meant so much to him. Can you imagine my pleasant surprise when Larry showed this faded old note to me? There had been a few times he had rediscovered it in the envelope where he had placed it, and he had just quietly put it away. I can't imagine why he didn't just discard it after so much time had passed. I definitely had not saved the paper on which he had written his address!

Larry shocked me with a special gift five years ago when I retired from a thirty- seven- year teaching career. He purchased a red convertible with a black top for me because I had joked for over thirty years that that was what I would drive when I retired from teaching. Upon discovering his plan, I tried to talk him out of his expensive, impractical gift. Surprisingly, this practical man I had grown old with would not change his mind because he thought he had discovered the perfect gift for me.

Even though I have enjoyed my convertible tremendously, the sentiment that matters the most to me today is remembering the times when I most needed my husband and he was there: the birth of our children, the deaths of close friends and family, health crises, and situations that brought great personal anguish. He has given me many gifts of real, lasting value throughout our marriage. The perfect gift I have received is Larry himself. We both believe the Lord put us together because He knew how much we would bless each other.

God continuously desires for us to sit with Him and seek His guidance upon our daily living. We can do this by studying His Word, praying with other believers, and worshipping Him with our hearts and souls. One of the most thrilling moments to me in the last few years has come in the midst of Larry and me putting our arms around each other and praying. No one can offer a more powerful prayer for you than someone who loves you deeply as a husband or wife, a member of your family, or a very close friend who shares your love for the Lord.

The Lord is the expert on matters of the heart and has His own sentimental collections. Postmarks that reveal His heart for us are found in Scripture. Psalm 56:8 tells us that He stores our tears in a bottle and Revelation 5:8 reveals that He places our prayers in golden bowls in heaven. No tears shed in love for others go unnoticed by the living God. I rejoice knowing God has a "keepsake" of those moments in bottles and golden bowls in heaven. I can't think of anything more precious for Him to keep than tears and prayers from us His children! Pretty cool stuff from our awesome God!

If someone you love is not meeting your requirements to make you feel special, give your need instead to the living God. He gave His only Son for us because He loves us so deeply. Experiencing the love that God has for us puts us in a secure enough place to let others be less than perfect in loving us. Celebrate God's love and heart for you! Praise Him! He is awesome!

No one loves you more than God. He gave His only Son for you.

Romans 5:3-4

We can rejoice, too, when we run into problems and trials, for we know that they are good for us—they help us to endure. And endurance develops strength of character in us, and character strengthens our confident expectation of salvation.

Romans 8:28

And we know that God causes everything to work together for the good of those who love God and are called according to hi purpose for them.

Revelation 21:5

And the one sitting on the throne said, "Look, I am making all things new."

CHAPTER SEVENTEEN

God's Postmarks in Troubled Times: The Tangled Kite String

The three hundred and fifty feet of kite string lay in a large tangled mess on the floor of our hotel room at the beach. A couple of hours earlier my twelve-year-old grandson, Brandon, full of happiness and anticipation, had been on the beach attempting to fly his new kite. It was a beautiful, windy day, and he had great expectations for a long maiden flight. However, after only a few minutes aloft, the strong wind ripped the cardboard roll of string from his hands. The kite, free of Brandon's control, flew off for a trip to an unknown destination. Dejected, Brandon took off in a desperate, hopeless search for it down the beach.

Surprisingly, someone from the balcony of our hotel had witnessed the entire event and shouted out to Brandon and gave him the location of the kite which had traveled much further down the beach. Retrieving his wayward kite, he returned to our room and disgustedly threw it down on the floor. All the string was now in a hopeless wad of knots and tangles. It would have to be replaced.

The day had begun in such a joyful way for the whole family. My husband and I were at the beach for a vacation with Brandon and his ten-year-old sister Alyssa. We had prayed fervently the day before for their young Uncle Quinn to be able to speak. Suffering from encephalitis, he had seizures which had caused him to lose the ability to breathe on his own, speak, walk, and eat without a feeding tube. It had been over two months since his wife Kimberly had heard his voice. Quinn and Kimberly had been married for only one year when Quinn suddenly became ill. We had petitioned the Lord to enable Quinn to speak to bring encouragement to both him and Kimberly. That morning we received an email telling us that he had spoken!

Tangled kite string could not quench the happiness and hope we all felt about our answered prayer. I sat on a bed in our hotel room and compulsively began to pull the string apart. My husband said "Don't worry with that mess, we will get some string when we return home." That was the voice of reason.

I heard a different voice in my spirit. The Holy Spirit was telling me that the tangled string symbolized Quinn's recovery by the healing touch of the Lord. He was going to completely restore him. I honestly didn't know if it would be possible to straighten out that much tangled string with hundreds of knots, and it probably would be an investment in futility. It might also seem irrational for a grandmother to attempt such a task in front of her young grandchildren. That was what my mind said. My spirit said, "Keep going. You are going to like the end results."

For the next two days when we returned to our room after our beach activities, I worked on my project. I soon realized that I needed to detach the string from the kite to be able to maneuver the cardboard roll through the loops of string that were not in tight knots. I later realized the symbolism of that act. Impossible situations are on their way to being resolved when we let go of them and turn them over to the Lord.

Occasionally a few inches of string would pull free, only to cause more tangles and knots in the rest of the string. Progress seemed so slow, and at times it seemed like the situation was getting worse instead of better. Yet, I could see more freed string accumulate on the cardboard roll. Occasionally, several inches would release and I would think, "Maybe this is possible after all!"

Sometimes I would come to a place where I felt I had reached a stopping point because of a knot that looked like it was too tight to pull loose. I would then insert the tip of a nail file to pry it free. It appeared impossible, but that was an illusion based on what my eyes perceived. As I continued I remembered witnessing faithful, bold prayers of others that were followed by miracles for situations that appeared to be devoid of hope. God was speaking to me through tangled string.

I continued to be amazed that despite all the tight maneuvering of the string, it didn't break. It was normal lightweight string you would use for securing balloons and kites. I recognized this as a good analogy of the human experience for believers. We are weak, but because the Lord's strength is in us through the Holy Spirit, we do not "break." He sustains us in perilous situations where we know our own energy and effort will not be enough.

On the last day of our vacation the last of the string untangled, and I was able to carefully rewind all the string back again onto the cardboard roll. Looking at it, one would never suspect that it had been in a horrible mess two days earlier.

I shared with my grandchildren the story of faith represented by the string and the process the Lord was using to untangle all the "knots" in Quinn's restoration process. Sometimes, progress would seem too slow. Hope would be dashed on some days, but God would not stop what He was doing in healing Quinn. I told them I believed Quinn would be made completely whole by the hand of the living God and his testimony would be mighty for Him. I believe that through the touch of the Lord's hand on Quinn's life many, many lives will be blessed.

Three years later, Quinn is still on his journey. He is walking, talking, eating, and playing his musical instruments. These are all miracles which looked totally impossible when he was first devastated by this terrible illness. This past Christmas our family received a card from Quinn and Kimberly with the title" Blessed: So much to be grateful for this holiday season." God is still at work to give this young man and his family an incredible testimony for His kingdom. It has come at a great price and its value cannot be measured by human standards, but God will take the cost and transform it again and again with treasured words of encouragement in the hearts of believers who hear of Quinn's story.

Are you or someone close to you going through a situation that appears to be devoid of hope and restoration? Remember the example of the tangled kite string when solutions to these trials in your life seem out of reach, and you have no expectation of victory. Oftentimes our situation appears impossible, and we fervently pray without seeing the answer we seek. Walk in faith and believe for what you cannot see. Give the living God time to loosen all the "knots" on His timeline. Praise God! Praise God!

When you are experiencing a trial in your life, remember God is working on your behalf on His timeline. Wait on Him.

Exodus 17: 8-13

While the people of Israel were still at Rephidim, the warriors of Amalek came to fight against them. Moses commanded Joshua, "Call the Israelites to arms, and fight the army of Amalek. Tomorrow, I will stand at the top of the hill with the staff of God in my hand."

So Joshua did what Moses had commanded. He led his men out to fight the army of Amalek. Meanwhile Moses, Aaron, and Hur went to the top of a nearby hill. As long as Moses held up the staff with his hands, the Israelites had the advantage. But whenever he lowered his hands, the Amalekites gained the upper hand. Moses' arms finally became too tired to hold up the staff any longer. So Aaron and Hur found a stone for him to sit on. Then they stood on each side, holding up his hands until sunset. As a result, Joshua and his troops were able to crush the army of Amalek.

Isaiah 64:4

For since the world began, no ear has heard, and no eye has seen a God like you, who works for those who wait for him!

CHAPTER EIGHTEEN

God's Postmarks in Hopeless Situations

*T*he small dogwood tree stood at the edge of our front yard for more than twenty-five years. It had always been bent at a steep angle to the ground, and its small trunk had slowly hollowed out so much that there now appeared to be very little support for keeping it in the ground. Its branches had born a few green leaves until the last couple of years but now the sad appearance of its present condition motivated my husband and me to discuss its removal.

We had been married for over forty years and had spent twenty-five of them in our present home. Every time we stopped our cars in the driveway to retrieve our mail from the mail box, the tree was nearby to greet us. I always found the tree to be a vision of comfort as I looked at the bent and mostly hollow trunk. This hopeless-looking tree somehow continued to stand without much visible support. Some friends politely suggested we should remove it. I always believed the Lord had left the tree in our yard as a postmark to remind us of what He can do in situations that seem impossible for desirable outcomes.

Only a few years earlier, my ninety-two-year-old mother had fallen at her home and broken her hip. She had been reasonably healthy and in bright spirits in recent times, and people had always been impressed with her remarkable spirit. No matter what burdens came her way over the years—the death of her nine-year-old son, the death of her husband of forty years, an automobile accident that hospitalized her, a mugging in front of a store which resulted in a broken hip, and the death of many of her friends—she continued to walk in her faith and prayers. Our dogwood tree reminded me of her. She had overcome her limited mobility and was again thriving at the age of ninety-three.

Our celebration of her ninetieth birthday at our church had been christened with an unexpected blanket of March snow. Mother's zest for life encouraged us to invite the few brave people who risked their well-being to attend this birthday party to come back in ten years for her hundredth birthday. She is a living tree of faith.

When my husband and I met with a landscaper, who was going to design a plan to restore our front and back yards, I asked him if we could focus on the tree as a cornerstone of the renovation project of the front yard. I explained to him that I considered the tree a postmark from the Lord, and it represented a symbol of faith in circumstances that did not seem to support that faith. Being afraid the tree would fall down before his return trip, he asked if we had anything we could use to support the tree. My husband then retrieved two pieces of lumber from our garage and put them in place under the failing tree.

The decision to preserve this possible postmark from the Lord was followed by some surprising events. A few days later, a neighbor who I rarely saw and had not spoken to in some time, saw me outside in the yard close to the tree and approached me. She offered some good natured questions about the boards placed under the tree.

I shared with her the symbolism I saw in the tree. After that conversation I also noticed two green shoots at the end of one of the branches which quickly disappeared as if the tree had taken its "last breath of life."

The landscaper returned a couple of weeks later, and his

eyes lit up when he unveiled his plans for the section of the yard surrounding the tree. He smiled as he said, "We will build a redwood pergola to place under the tree for support and plant a flowering vine at the base which will bring life to the tree as it grows upward around it. We will also set a stone bench under the pergola to provide a place for prayer and meditation." After these plans were implemented, I placed two small angel figurines on each side of the bench.

Later, as I reflected on this new addition to our yard, I realized the Lord was giving me another message through the failing tree. Many times during the previous few years I had shared a particular story in the Bible with people struggling to win their personal battles. I recounted the story of Moses who was standing on a nearby hill during a battle. He held a staff in the air while the Israelites fought against the attacking Amalekites. When his arms were up, the Israelites were winning the war, but when he became tired and put his arms down the Israelites began to lose. Aaron and Hur, who were nearby, found a stone for Moses to sit on. They stood on each side of him and held up his hands until the battle was won.

The symbolism of the stone bench under the tree and the pergola which replaced the two supporting pieces of wood gave me renewed inspiration! The story of Moses is a message desperately needed today in our battles against our enemy—Satan. We need the support of God's Word in our search for life and restoration of what has been lost.

I recently recounted this story to a young couple who were struggling in their marriage. I told them that if they would regularly seek the Lord in a house of worship and patiently join their hands in daily prayer for each other, I believed the Lord would save their marriage. I believe that prayer and worship have strengthened the marriages of many believers.

I know when couples wrap their arms around each other and pray, the enemies they face fall back in defeat. When my husband was baptized and joined our church several years ago, a great blessing came upon our marriage. For the first time, we wrapped our arms around each other in prayer when we faced times of great distress or opportunities of testimony for the Lord. We prayed before he went to the hospital for cancer surgery, we prayed when our daughter was close to death before a miracle came, we prayed at his mother's bedside as she lay dying, and we prayed in celebration as he began an unexpected ministry in music and I published my first Christian book. We worshipped together in our church, and the Lord gave us new joy and celebration that drenched our spirits with His presence.

The dogwood tree recently fell apart, and I found the remnants scattered in our yard. I had just hired an artist to draw the tree for the cover of this book, and he had spent many hours sketching the tree to accurately reflect its story. I like to believe that the timing of the tree's failure until after this last recording of its presence in our yard was a sign from the Lord that he was blessing this testimony.

A new tree has now been planted, and the meditation area with the stone bench, pergola, and plants remain. This area would never have existed if the failing tree had not inspired it. When I finished writing this chapter we were in the mountains, and my husband excitedly noticed another confirmation for what I had just composed. He said, "I don't know what you have just written, but it must be pretty good! Look outside our living room window!" We saw the biggest and closest rainbow that we had ever observed. It hung close to the deck of the house where we were staying. I believe the Lord was repeating a promise of hope that He knew I would share with others.

Our Father tells us to wait on Him to act on our behalf (Isaiah 64:4). He is ready to perform His will in our lives for His glory and honor! We live in an age of great love of self and forgetfulness of who we are as God's children. Our hearts are crying out for urgent needs of prayer, worship, knowledge of God's Word, and the grace and patience to wait on Him!

Do you need support as you have become tired and can no longer hold up your hands in prayer by yourself? Do you need an Aaron and Hur to help you win a battle that threatens to bring defeat? Stay in God's Word and worship Him for who He is. Pray with others and it will help keep you and them close to the Lord. If you sit on God's Word as your stone of support, you will walk in victory! Wait on the living God and let him fight on your behalf. He will bring a blessing on your life that will touch not only you but also the lives of everyone around you. May your testimony bring honor and glory to the living God!

Do you need support from God? While you wait on Him, stay in His word, worship Him, and pray with others.

Exodus 23:20

"See, I am sending an angel before you to protect you on your journey and lead you safely to the place I have prepared for you."

Psalm 91:11-12

For he orders his angels to protect you wherever you go. They will hold you with their hands to keep you from striking your foot on a stone.

Psalm 34:7

For the angel of the LORD is a guard; he surrounds and defends all who fear him.

Isaiah 58:8-9

"If you do these things, your salvation will come like the dawn. Yes, your healing will come quickly. Your godliness will lead you forward, and the glory of the LORD will protect you from behind. Then when you call, the LORD will answer. 'Yes, I am here,' he will quickly reply."

CHAPTER NINETEEN

God Uses Angels for Postmarks Of His Presence

*R*ain was drenching the concrete driveway when they noticed something extraordinary—there were four pairs of "arches" where the rain seemed to be invisible. Those regions, which ranged in size from only a couple of feet to six feet across, were absolutely dry in the middle of a downpour. They began to appear every time it rained. Trusting that angels were always around them inspired the family to identify the "arches" as the outer part of angels' wings. They believed the angels were camped out in those areas keeping the rain from touching the concrete.

When the concrete was newly poured, replacing an old gravel road to the house, I had prayed over my friends' house, surrounding buildings, and had sprinkled anointing oil in several places on the driveway. I asked the Lord to send guardian angels to protect the family against any harm, and I recognized these inexplicable dry surfaces as a postmark for this answered prayer.

After the heartbreaking loss of a family member, who was in his early forties, a fifth arched area appeared in the driveway when it rained. The family believed God sent them this sign to comfort them. The story of this family member's miraculous birth had been told many times as a testimony for the Lord. His mother had been eight months pregnant with him when she died on the way to the hospital. Even though several minutes had elapsed before her arrival at the hospital, a doctor performed a Caesarean section. At first the delivery of this baby appeared to be an additional tragedy for the family. His color was extremely dark, and he appeared not to be breathing. Even after he took his first breaths the doctor feared that this tiny, motherless baby had experienced severe brain damage. He was wrong. By the grace of God he led a blessed life as a son, husband, father and follower of Jesus Christ.

Whenever a believer steps into a building or home and experiences inexplicable comfort, it may be a sign that God has placed His angels at that location. Several years ago when I was teaching at an elementary school, another teacher and I regularly prayed for angels to walk the halls to protect and inspire the administrators, teachers and students. People would frequently enter the building and comment that there was something special about the school. Later, during a very stressful school year, teachers would gather en masse before the school day to pray. Occasionally a teacher would rise out of her seat before a faculty meeting and spontaneously offer prayer. Hearing about these happenings made me wonder if an atmosphere for prayer began when the building was newly built and a Christian principal stepped into the building for the first time. Perhaps his faith anointed this school for God's work, and God sent His angels to watch over the children and adults who walked those halls.

A few years after I left this school, my daughter was hired to teach there. Before the school year began, she and I prayed over every desk, window, and doorway of her classroom, and every time I visited this room during the school year I felt a special, sweet presence. I sensed angels were there to protect and bless the children, my daughter, and others who entered. The joy and countenance of the students reflected the special atmosphere of that classroom.

God has an amazing love for us and is always sending signs of His presence to give us joy, comfort, and strength. Several years ago in one of the women's Bible studies at my church, we searched Scripture to learn about the glory of the Lord. We also did research about the role of archangels in God's work on Earth. We discovered that they are the highest ranking angels in heaven and deliver messages from God to human beings. Empowered by God's Word, and taking new steps in our faith walk, we prayed for Him to show us His glory during the week. A few days later one of the ladies found a white feather next to her mail box, and one sunny day that same week I looked into the sky and recognized that two clouds had the shape of two large angels! A silent message came into my spirit revealing to me I was looking at archangels. I joyfully shared these observations with our Bible study ladies the next time we met. The synchronization of these sightings with our prayer request convinced all of us that our heavenly Father had given us a postmark for our group.

The story of the prophet Elisha, having been protected by God's angels, is told in vivid detail in 2 Kings, Chapter 16. The King of Aram sent a great army to kill Elisha, and when Elisha's servant went outside their home one morning, he saw enemy troops, horses, and chariots everywhere. Elisha told the disbelieving servant not to worry about what he saw. He said that there was a much more powerful army present to ensure their safety. Elisha asked God to reveal to his servant what he was seeing, and at that point the servant looked up and saw a hillside filled with horses and chariots of fire sent by the living God. The story proceeds with the enemy suddenly leaving.

In many places in the Old Testament we read that God sent angels to let His people know they were not alone in their battles against the enemy. However, in several other places we read that God's anointed prophets and saints did not always have divine physical protection. They experienced much suffering and died at the hands of evil people. As believers, how do we reconcile these differences?

Today in the challenging world we live in, we often see this same lack of divine protection from tragedy. We ask where God and His angels were when suffering comes to our loved ones, friends, and even strangers in the news who grab our heart strings. They die of disease, accidents, and on battlefields. A former FBI agent told her story of seeing hundreds and hundreds of angels and archangels at the plane crash site in Shanksville, Pennsylvania on September 11, 2001. We know that some of the passengers on this flight acted heroically to save the lives of other people. The terrorists on this plane did not reach their intended destination to destroy perhaps hundreds of lives in our nation's capital, Washington D.C. Critics who heard about this agent's story asked why the angels did not intervene and save the people on that doomed plane before it crashed. Perhaps the living God sent His angels because the crash site had become anointed ground. The agent was the only person to see these angels and for all who accepted her words, comfort from the hand of God was given.

No one can answer for God why so many good people, who are desperately needed by their families, die before they have lived long lives. Yet there are many reports of believers having miraculous sightings of angels and the interventions of invisible angels in the midst of tragedy. I trust God's love for His people and accept that all explanations reside in His glory unfolding on this earth.

Isaiah in Chapter 58, verses 8 and 9 describes the behavior of Godly people and tells us that if we exhibit these qualities, our godliness will lead us forward, and the glory of the Lord will protect us from behind. When we have arrived at our home in heaven, I believe there will be many stories from our angels telling us of all the times they stepped in to protect us from harm. We may also learn of tragedies that came upon our loved ones that were transformed into enormous victories when they stepped into the presence of the living God.

Believe God for your future. He will bring you into a resounding victory when you arrive in heaven and dwell eternally with Him! When we call, the Lord will tell us that He is there. I believe God's angels are part of the protection He provides for our rear guard. Sometimes victory is dramatic and visible and we celebrate what our eyes have witnessed. On other occasions we search without seeing these amazing results. Don't give up too soon! There are times when victory is assured for the future and does not reside in the present. Continue to believe, trust God and walk in His footprints.

Believe God for your future. Don't give up too soon! Trust God and walk in His footprints.

Hebrews 12:1

Therefore, since we are surrounded by such a huge crowd of witnesses to the life of faith, let us strip off every weight that slows us down, especially the sin that so easily hinders our progress. And let us run with endurance the race that God has set before us.

1 Corinthians 9:24-25

Remember that in a race everyone runs, but only one person gets the prize. You also must run in such a way that you will win. All athletes practice strict self-control. They do it to win a prize that will fade away, but we do it for an eternal prize.

CHAPTER TWENTY

God's Postmark in An Unexpected Family Reunion

*W*e sat in a circle in my Uncle Gordon's living room laughing and sharing memories of years long past. Sadly my Aunt Francis had passed away several years previously, but we were enjoying our time with my uncle. We were there with his second wife of only a few years, my uncle's son and his wife, two other cousins and their spouses, and my husband. It was a reunion that none of us thought possible only a year before. My ninety-two year old uncle had been hospitalized with failing kidneys and many other age-related physical difficulties.

About a year previously, a cousin and I, together with our husbands, had traveled from different locations to meet at my cousin's vacation home in Florida for our annual visit. We made plans on our last day there to visit our beloved uncle who was in a hospital two hours away. When we arrived, we anxiously searched for his room only to learn that Uncle Gordon had been taken to another location in the hospital for a lengthy procedure. Dejectedly we left with the knowledge that due to his prognosis and advanced age, we might never see him again.

Yet here we sat a year later receiving an unanticipated gift from the Lord. Even though my uncle could not recall the names of his nieces and nephews, the light in his eyes was as vibrant as any of us could remember. Someone had given him a stuffed "talking" parrot a few years earlier, and joy "sneaked up" on us as we played with it and interacted with him.

This reunion was the last time most of us saw Uncle Gordon. He left this world a few months later to go to be with the Lord in his eternal home. God had simply given my cousin, her husband, my husband and me a second chance to enjoy his company. We understood that and savored our time with him. We are not despondent in our sorrow of losing him to death because we look forward to seeing him again when our time on earth is finished. Until my life is over, I pray I will be able to share his testimony with other family members, my circle of friends, and strangers who come my way.

My uncle always seemed to be able to capture joy and receive the daily pleasures life offers. Over fifty years ago when he and my aunt were in their forties, they realized an unexpected seventh child was on the way. They accepted this event as part of God's plan for their lives. I remember as a twelve-year-old child visiting them and hearing my uncle say as he held the new baby, "Not every house in our town has the gift of a new baby!" Love resided in Uncle Gordon and Aunt Francis' home. They filled it with the harmony of music resonating from lives well-lived, as well as from several musical instruments they purchased for their children, and a multitude of prayers.

After serving in World War II, my uncle had a very long and successful career as an electrical engineer for a company based in Wisconsin. He even held patents in the area of electrical generator controls. His consulting opportunities took him all over the United States and the around the world. It was obvious to all his family and friends that he was a brilliant man, but he covered his superior mind with humility. No one was ever made to feel that his intelligence was inferior by comparison. When people spoke to him, he looked into their eyes and seemed to enjoy the conversation wherever it led. In the last few years of my aunt's life, he became a loving and tender caregiver honoring her in the last days of a sixty-year marriage.

Uncle Gordon and Aunt Francis had been devoted to their church. Their years of heartfelt worship remain a lasting witness to the entire family. My uncle taught Sunday school and Bible classes for many years. Only in the last few years of his life did he relinquish giving this blessing to others. He was a member of a runners club and participated in Senior Olympics, receiving a national senior gold medal. Just as his ability to run and compete in races until his late eighties spoke to the family about his retention of youthful characteristics, his passion for running his race for the Lord still resonates with so many who were given this witness. Occasionally he received attention from the local newspaper about his racing events, giving the opportunity for his inspiration to reach total strangers.

Although the wonderful, cherished moments of time spent with my uncle were way too few, they still dwell in my spirit and thoughts. They challenge any temptation I have to grieve about my own age. I have lived to be a senior citizen. I only realize the full extent of that fact when I look into the mirror or come too quickly to the end of my endurance in the midst of a physical task. Uncle Gordon's spirit remained young all his life. His body's time to be on Earth came to an end so he could reach his full potential in the presence of the Lord.

Resolve to never grow old in spirit and finish your "race" with courage, hope and faith for the promises the living God has made to all who believe in His Son. These promises were sealed with the cross and resurrection of our Lord Jesus Christ. Remember, you run your race not only for your own benefit but also for the benefit of others who see Christ reflected in your life.

Run your race with courage, hope, and faith for yourself and others.

Psalm 119:133

Guide my steps by your word, so I will not be overcome by any evil.

Proverbs 16:9

We can make our plans but the LORD determines our steps.

Psalm 37:23-24

The steps of the godly are directed by the LORD. He delights in every detail of their lives. Though they stumble, they will not fall, for the LORD holds them by the hand.

CHAPTER TWENTY-ONE

God's Postmarks: Footprints from the Past Leading to the Future

*M*y friend held out her hand to reveal the beautiful jeweled antique-looking watch, and then looking into my eyes, she slowly placed it in my hand. Its value was too great to be measured for it had been worn by her mother who was no longer living.

Just a couple of years previously, my friend had admired it when I wore it and inquired where she might buy one like it. Even though her mother was suffering greatly in the last months of her life, she still enjoyed wearing jewelry and watches. The stretchable, bracelet watch was new but made to look like a vintage piece of jewelry. Knowing it was probably no longer available to purchase, I slipped the watch off my wrist and handed it to my friend. I knew the greatest pleasure I could receive would not be in wearing it but in giving it to her cherished mother.

A few months had passed since her mother's death, and now my friend was giving the watch back to me. As I slipped it on my wrist I noticed it was slightly larger. I smiled as I realized that, because it had been worn on the larger wrist of a woman of great faith, it had been transformed into an incredible treasure for me.

I had been privileged on occasion to pray with my friend's mother when she sought freedom from her suffering, and she frequently told me that when I prayed for her she experienced relief. It had nothing to do with me, but everything to do with her tremendous faith and the grace of the living God. When she did not experience immediate release from her pain, she continued to praise God and believe she was still held in His hands. This watch that had once been on her wrist gave me a sweet connection to her even though she was no longer living.

I believe that sometimes God gives us a special blessing when we come into possession of something that once belonged to a loved one who has left this world. Certainly my maternal grandmother's rolling pin is a superb example of this sentiment. I remember when I was a child she used it to make Christmas cookies with one of my favorite cousins, Mary Dell, and me. I can still see the three of us making sugar cookies and piling them high with decorative icing and sprinkles until they broke apart from the weight. Today, I use this same rolling pin to make cookies with my grandchildren, and I always remind them that their Great-Great Grandmother Overstreet used it with me. I place their hands where her hands had once lain on the rolling pin knowing her blessing upon my life is being passed to other generations.

My Grandmother Overstreet was a woman of great faith, and in her later years she taught Sunday school to a group of seventy-five to one hundred adults. She had many talents, including that of an artist. She gave me a painting a few years before her death, but it was some time before I realized exactly what I had been given. I had to mature in my own faith walk to grasp the meaning of the painting and comprehend the message she was passing on to me. The picture she had beautifully represented with her brush strokes was Abraham leading Isaac to offer a sacrifice to God. The animal standing beside them was carrying wood to be burned on the altar where Abraham was to place his beloved son. This picture illustrated one of the greatest demonstrations of faith the living God has ever given, and revealed what God did for us when He sacrificed his only

Son.

Recently, my ninety-four-year-old mother passed on to me three of her prized treasures knowing I would recognize their value. As I held them in my hands, I went back in time over sixty years when I was only seven years old and my nine-year-old brother died. I tenderly rubbed my fingers over the yarn slippers that had once been on my brother's feet, turned the pages of his coloring book seeing where his fingers had once held crayons, and held his small handmade baseball. I had not realized that mother had sought comfort all these years from Bobby's things. Holding them in my hands made me remember what it was like to have a brother. I have a picture of the two of us sitting in his red wagon which was taken a few months before he died, and my spirit went back to that time as if it was yesterday.

After experiencing this devastating loss, my family courageously continued to worship God and lean on the prayers of others for their healing. Even though their prayers for my brother's healing had not been answered in the way their aching hearts had pleaded, they continued to believe. They walked the same footprints of faith that had been laid for them by Abraham, David, and other "spiritual giants" of the Bible. They walked the path our Lord laid down for all believers when he dwelled on this earth.

I seek to continue this journey and leave footprints of faith for my children and grandchildren. Indeed I still have the hand prints of my two adult children which were made when they were about the age of six and seven. Even though they are now in their forties, seeing these imprints on cloth and ceramic clay take me back to when they were children and I was striving to teach them about our Lord. Now they are on the same journey with their own children who currently range in age from three to sixteen.

One of my granddaughters, who is fourteen, accidentally had her footprints embedded on a beautiful, hand-painted chest in my foyer when she was about four years old. One day when my daughter was visiting, she placed Alyssa's very inexpensive rubber soled shoes on it and asked me to keep them at my house as a spare pair of shoes for when she visited. They stayed there for a few days, and when I lifted them to put them away, the place where the soles of the shoes had made contact left an imprint. At first I was distraught to see this nice piece of furniture marred by the shoes, and then I realized that God had made a "memorial stone" for my granddaughter. Someday this piece of furniture will take its place in her home when she is married and has children of her own. I pray that she will continue to seek God's footprints in guiding her own family to know the Lord and walk in His ways.

Just as we can touch what our loved ones have once owned to revive a memory of the past or weave a connection for the future, we can do the same thing with our heavenly Father. We can hold a deceased loved one's possessions in our hands for comfort, and we can hold God's Word in our hearts and feel comfort from the Holy Spirit. We can "touch" what the living God Himself has "touched" by reading His Word and storing it in our minds, hearts, and spirits. We can experience what God's authors of the Bible felt when He touched their spirits with divine inspiration. Surely they were blessed with God's breath upon their lives as their hands wrote His very Words. We can experience this same blessing when we receive His guidance for our faith journey.

It is God's Spirit that brings comfort to us in our times of greatest need to let us know that He is on the job. He is there right beside you, waiting for you to experience His love and touch upon your life. God has left His footprints in His Word for all believers that we may know Him. It is this "postmark" which He has given to lead us from the past to the future we will have with Him in our heavenly home. Be full of joy knowing that He is waiting there for us!

God has left His footprints in His Word so that you may know Him.

Revelation 21:5-7

And the one sitting on the throne said, "Look, I am making all things new!" And then he said to me, "Write this down, for what I tell you is trustworthy and true." And he also said "It is finished! I am the Alpha and the Omega—the Beginning and the End. To all who are thirsty I will give the springs of the water of life without charge!"

1 Corinthians 16: 13-14

Be on guard. Stand firm in the faith. Be courageous. Be strong. And do everything with love.

2 Corinthians 5:17

What this means is that those who become Christians become new persons. They are not the same anymore, for the old life is gone. A new life has begun!

CHAPTER TWENTY-TWO

A Postmark from the Hand of The Carpenter:
Rebirth and Restoration

A beautiful sight awaits me when I enter my sunroom. Sitting in front of the fireplace is a wooden hand-made wagon with four unique matching wheels. Two poinsettias reside in the plant holders inside the wagon and a much larger poinsettia rests beside it. I can't believe these plants are still thriving and blooming after so much time in my home. Some people are gifted with what we call a "green thumb" because they can make any plant thrive in their homes and gardens. I have what some call a "black thumb!" I usually purchase poinsettia plants every Christmas, and after a couple of months of my over-watering or forgetting to water them at all, they expire in "quiet desperation" and their leaves fall off. I always give them a "proper burial" in my trash can and accept the reality that they were meant to be a part of my life for only a short time.

These three poinsettias have managed to thrive in spite of me! Two of them have survived three Christmases in my home, and the newcomer has been with me since the Christmas of 2012. At one point in time I came close to discarding the plants after they began to take on the appearance of "near death." Sur-

prisingly, several weeks later, they gave evidence of new life
and had totally green leaves until about a month before this
past Christmas. Then suddenly they came alive with beautiful
red leaves as Jesus' birthday came near.

The wagon, which is the home of these plants, was made
by my brother-in-law, John, who is a retired teacher, a talented
carpenter, and a devout Christian. John built the wagon for me
one Christmas twenty years ago after I admired the one he had
made for my mother-in-law who is no longer with us. He and
my sister-in-law live over five hundred miles from our home,
and so our visits are infrequent. We were home for Christmas
that year with the family, and when we were preparing to open
presents, I noticed a huge box under the tree with no name. I
was thrilled when this gift was presented to me and I discovered the wagon inside. I couldn't believe John had set aside all
the hours required to make something so special for me. The
joy of that memory is still with me waiting to be recalled when
I need a lifted spirit.

I have learned that often when something unexpected or
unusual happens, it is the Lord giving me a sign that He is near.
So I began to ponder the message of a Christian carpenter of
deep faith, whose Bible is always nearby, making a wooden
wagon which houses plants that survive against the odds.

Recently, the wagon, lovingly built for my mother-in-law
so long ago, made the trip from its original home in Indiana to
find a new place in my daughter's home in Georgia. Now Jennifer has her uncle's handiwork in her home. She not only has
the same sentimental reminder that I have of that time many
years ago, she has another special connection by knowing the
message of the carpenter.

Jennifer was with me years ago when I received my hand-
built wagon, and she remembers it as vividly as I do. Sentimental attachments sometimes stir memories of events or situations that happened many years previously. These wonderful
memories then take on special new meaning for us. My brother-in-law has provided many opportunities for that to happen
in our family. He has made numerous gifts from wood to give
to friends and family members. A wooden cross John crafted
with my name imprinted on it resides in my prayer room. John
made it so others could pray over it before it was presented

to me after a Christian retreat over ten years ago! This hand-made cross continues to bring me great comfort when I hold it today.

It is, however, John's testimony for the Lord that has meant the most to all of us who know him. John has been the "glue" for our family over the years when many challenging situations were presented. Since my husband, Larry, and I have lived so far away he and my sister-in-law Lana have been on the "front line" when there were crisis events involving elderly parents and other family members who lived near them. He has remained constant in his faith walk, character, and voice of reason.

On one occasion a few years ago we were with John and Lana when a "gut wrenching" event took place involving a loved one back home in Georgia. I felt helpless and carried the weight of great anxiety when John interpreted what had happened through the lens of his faith. He said that perhaps God was working through the tears and heartbreak to bring good, not evil. His words: "Perhaps, God interceded to save him" resonate in my spirit today when adverse experiences come my way. After he shared his gift of discernment, my husband and I joined hands as John led the four of us in prayer.

John's words grasped the truth, and great healing and unexpected joy came to replace the darkness we were seeing on the day of that prayer. Our family experienced new growth and life which were beyond our expectations and hope. The prophecy given by John was a postmark for the future as God wove the tapestry of events together.

I love knowing that Jesus was a carpenter by trade and built many things from pieces of wood. How I would have loved to have seen and held some of the objects our Savior built with His hands! The New Testament gives testimony of many miracles of healing from our Lord's hands when they rested on hurting people. The Carpenter who built new things made people new in their bodies and spirits.

New growth and restoration are the postmarks the Lord always promises to us! When the Lord puts His healing hands on situations, relationships, health concerns, and the moments in our lives which challenge us to our core, new life and brand new possibilities evolve. Just as wood shavings fall away as a carpenter builds and refines his work, we have experiences that are part of our being shaped into who God meant for us to be. The hand of The Carpenter is upon our lives to renew us and bring life and even defy expectations of defeat and permanent loss of joy. He makes us new and His countenance is upon our lives! Praise Him! Praise the living God!

Seek the Lord and ask Him to place His healing hands on you to restore you and give you the newness life.

Romans 3:21-22

But now God has shown us a different way of being right in his sight—not by obeying the law but by the way promised in the Scriptures long ago. We are made right in God's sight when we trust in Jesus Christ to take away our sins. And we all can be saved in this same way, no matter who we are or what we have done.

Romans 8:38*

For I am convinced that neither death nor life, neither angels nor demons, neither the present nor the future, nor any powers, neither height nor depth, nor anything else in all creation, will be able to separate us from the love of God that is in Christ Jesus our Lord.

Ephesians 1:13

And now you also have heard the truth, the Good News that God saves you. And when you believed in Christ, he identified you as his own by giving you the Holy Spirit, whom he promised long ago.

*NIV

CHAPTER TWENTY-THREE

God's Best Postmark: His Seal of Approval

The eighty-year-old woman gave her answer in a voice that conveyed great sadness, "I don't know." We were sitting in a small circle in a group meeting at a church retreat, and the leader had just asked the question for each of us to ponder: "If you were to die this very day, do you know with complete certainty that you would go to heaven?" This lady had just spoken of being raised in the church and faithfully attending church all her life. Yet she could not speak with conviction about her future in eternity. The leader cautiously asked if he could guide her through the question again with the Bible he held in his hand. She spoke with uneasiness when she said, "Another time would be better to pursue this question."

I was surprised with her response, because I had known her and her family for many years. I had prayed with the family when they experienced a recent shocking death of a loved one. I believed faith was the vital ingredient in their lives sustaining them through their deep, penetrating grief. I carried a heavy burden with me as I returned home that day.

This experience lingered in my spirit in such a profound way that I approached my teenage grandson, Brandon, a few days later with the same penetrating question. "If you were to die today, do you know that you will go to heaven?" His answer stunned me. He said, "I don't think anyone can say that they are definitely going to heaven when they die."

I was at Brandon's side a few years earlier when he had heard the recorded testimony of University of Georgia football coach Mark Richt. I had put it in the car CD player before I arrived at his house to take him to his piano lesson. We listened to it as we traveled the twenty minute journey to our destination. After we returned back to his home, even though we were sitting in darkness, he refused to leave the car until he had heard the entire message. I had believed for many years that Brandon knew the Lord as his Savior, but after hearing Coach Richt offer the invitation to pray to accept Jesus as Lord of your life, I asked him if he had ever prayed that prayer. He said "No." I responded with my own invitation to pray that prayer with him. I will never forget sitting in my car with him as he made this commitment to the Lord. Surely, thousands of angels in the heavens rejoiced as they heard Brandon's spoken words.

Later, I felt pure exhilaration as I remembered those precious minutes with my grandson. I pondered this joyous thought, "I can die and go home to be with Jesus now that I have experienced the blessing of being with a grandchild as he made an eternal covenant with the living God!" Even though Brandon had shown knowledge of the Lord and had been a prayer warrior since the age of nine, he had never before prayed to accept Jesus into his life as Lord and Savior. Several months later, he participated in the confirmation class at our church and gave his pledge to become a member. He was so proud of this milestone in his life, and all our family were filled with enormous joy that very special day.

Even with these spiritual footsteps taken in his faith journey, my treasured grandson had not been able to name without any doubts the location of his eternal home. I am wondering how many believers have a lingering doubt about where they will be when their earthly bodies are finished. As for me, my reservation is booked, and I have accepted this reservation to go home to be with the Lord. When asked the question, "If you were to die this very day, do you know with complete certainty that you will go to heaven?" My answer is "I am already there!" In my spirit I am living eternal life with my Lord, and when my body dies I will transition to my real home.

My belief about my future destination is based on much more than optimism and hope. Righteousness from God came to me through my faith in Jesus Christ when I became a believer, and although I know that I am thoroughly and completely a sinner, I am justified by God's grace through the redemption of Jesus Christ (Romans 3: 21-22). I am guilty of my sins, but Jesus paid the price for me and washed me in His blood. Not only am I a new, clean, and restored person in Christ, His Spirit is in me. His Holy Spirit came to reside in me when I repented of my sins and accepted Him as my Lord and Savior. (Ephesians 1:13/ Galatians 4:6)

A Christian friend once said to me, "I hope that when we die we do not exist in oblivion until Christ returns to Earth." I told her, "I do not believe that is possible. Christ's Spirit dwells in us and because He is there, we can never be without His presence!" Romans 8:38 gives us the beautiful words of certainty that there is absolutely no earthly circumstance or power that can separate us from the living God. Nothing can get between believers and their Lord, Jesus Christ. Where He is, we are also right beside Him. I know my Redeemer lives in heaven and in me, and when my earthly body is finished I will reside in heaven with Him.

After reflecting on these thoughts, I shared them with my grandson, and a huge smile appeared on his face as he received the message and realized with certainty the location of his eternal home. My words were not my own. They were offered from God's Word. His Word penetrates our hearts and gives us assurance that cannot come from any earthly source!

My assignment from the Lord for the rest of my days is to let others hear this message and pray for them to accept the victorious message that God writes on believers' hearts. God's seal of approval is given to us when we accept Jesus as our Lord and Savior. This is the very best postmark He has given to let us know He is "on the job and working for us" so that we might live abundantly victorious lives. Praise Him! Praise Him.

God's seal of approval is yours when you accept Jesus as your Lord and Savior.

Isaiah 52:12*

For you shall not go out with haste, nor go by flight; For the LORD will go before you and the God of Israel will be your rear guard.

Isaiah 40:5*

Then the glory of the LORD will be revealed, and all the people will see it together. The LORD has spoken!

*ESV

CHAPTER TWENTY-FOUR

God's Postmarks in the Midst of Tragedy

"Gogo! The angel's wings were so soft!" Those were the words of a little seven-year-old boy who had just survived a deadly automobile accident. Tristan was telling his grandmother why he had not been injured in the horrific accident that had taken the life of his father's best friend. The three of them had been returning from a joyous fishing trip when the driver, Michael, ran a stop sign. Michael was now dead but the little boy's father, Adam, was still conscious and lying on the side of the road with terrible, painful injuries. Their car had been hit by another automobile after which it had rolled over three or four times and was now mangled and crushed. The emergency crew had used the "jaws of life" to extract all three victims. Indeed, they had opened the top of the car and peeled it back to retrieve the two men and the little boy. In a sequence of miracles, the driver of the other car was not seriously injured.

"Gogo" is the nickname given to my friend Gloria by many family members. Gloria had just arrived at the scene and knelt next to her son Adam. She was later told by admissions personnel at the hospital that Adam probably had internal injuries, a broken neck, ruptured spleen and a broken leg. There was also much concern about brain damage because the young man had experienced head trauma and could not hear. He later recounted to his family that during the accident, there was a loud, deafening explosion, and his head had repeatedly hit violently against his friend's head.

Gloria could also see a huge gaping wound on Adam's leg which would probably require many stitches and perhaps extensive surgery. When the paramedics placed a brace on this leg it would not close because the leg was so swollen and twisted. Gloria had seen many miraculous healings in her family, so she instinctively laid her hands on Adam and began to pray. As she prayed with great fervor and emotion, she felt heat radiating from her hands as she moved them over her son's body. She stopped praying aloud only when Adam was placed in the ambulance, and she then continued her urgent pleading with the Lord as her husband frantically drove them to the hospital.

When they reached the emergency room they were told that Adam was being prepared for surgery and that X-rays and a CT scan had been ordered. The results from these tests revealed surprising results—there were no fractures or internal injuries. After the brace was removed it was discovered that the leg had straightened and the huge, open wound on the leg, which had been bleeding profusely at the scene of the accident, had miraculously closed and no stitches would be required. The emergency room nurse was heard to say, "I guess God is still in the miracle business."

Even so, there was much bruising and swelling of Adam's body to be dealt with. Throughout all that had happened God revealed His presence in several miraculous ways. When Adam's clothing was removed, the imprint of a very large hand was found on his left shoulder which was opposite to where his seat belt had been. It would seem that it was not physically possible for his friend to have placed his hand on Adam's shoulder during the accident, leaving only one answer for how this impression on his flesh had been created. There was someone else present during the accident! I believe this was the angel who Tristan spoke about.

Several weeks of recovery were required for Adam's physical

injuries to heal. A year later an x-ray revealed another miracle-a neck fracture, not identified at the time of the original work-up after the accident, had miraculously healed. Many years of God's touch on Adam would be needed for his spirit to heal. Losing his best friend in such a horrible way would impact his life in ways which would cause him to never again be the same person. Profound loss has a way of doing this to people who love others so very deeply. However, Adam's pain will not be in vain for God has a journey for him that will weave this tragedy into testimony.

Five years later, Tristan still talks about the soft angel wings he encountered during the accident. One young man died, another survived with miraculous healing, and one little boy survived without even a scratch. God sent His angel to be at that accident with all three occupants of the car. Why then did Michael leave this earth? No one can answer that question, but faith tells us to wait and endure the stinging sorrow left behind. God does not ask us to experience devastating pain such as this alone. He is right there beside us, and as we reach for His comforting touch, He strengthens us.

Our profound grief after the death of a loved one inhabits every fiber of our emotional being. It has been over sixty years since my nine-year-old brother died, but I can still see my father sitting in his chair in the living room after the funeral. I had never seen tears in my father's eyes before that day, but his shoulders were heaving as he sobbed over the loss of his only son. He had prayed fervently and asked God to heal Bobby, but he died anyway.

My father was a teacher, and when I also entered the profession we frequently talked about what God had done in us through the grief we shared. We had a great compassion for children, especially for those who had serious physical and emotional needs. Reaching out to touch those students somehow brought us healing and made us feel more connected to our Lord. He had allowed us to walk through the valley of despair to temper our spirits in a way that would make us more loving vessels for His children. God touched our students through our hands, minds, and spirits. Our painful strands of sorrow were woven into compassion that spontaneously sprung forth when it was needed.

I can still remember my father speaking to one of my friends, a former student of his, after she lost her four-year-old son. He could reach her and comfort her in a way that only came from having walked the same road of grief. God used my father's pain to be a blessing to this grieving mother. It cost my father a lot to be eligible to be used by God in a way he had not chosen. God knew the price, because He had paid it Himself, and in the most incredible act of love ever seen in the history of man—God chose to sacrifice His Beloved Son to save us.

Several years ago my husband lost a favorite cousin as a result of a one-car accident on a slippery road. Linda was a beautiful, vivacious woman in her forties and left a grieving husband, two adult daughters and two adoring parents. Surely, she had much life yet to be lived. She was an ardent believer and had expressed great concern about her parents no longer attending church. The night she died she miraculously appeared to her father. He tells an incredible story; "As I sat in my living room sobbing with grief that bore open my very soul, she came to me. I saw her in full body form as if she were still alive. She told me not to cry because she was in a much better place." After this vision her father and mother again became avid church-goers. The Lord had given them a powerful message about eternal life, and they knew how blessed they were to know without any doubt that they would see their daughter again when they also arrived at their true home.

God's postmarks in tragedy often look different when seen through the eyes of each person who actually experiences such tragic events. God sometimes delivers us from the darkness, sometimes through the darkness, and sometimes He delivers us to Himself. Michael was delivered into His hands, and we can never know or explain why his life on earth ended this way. We do know that heaven is the real home for all believers, and people who have had near-death experiences describe it to be so awesome and beautiful they did not want to leave and return to their earthly home. No amount of earthly joy or misery can deny us the promise that our Lord has given us—the best is yet to come!

When we reach our heavenly home and reside with the living God, we will experience the victory that Michael and Linda did on the day of their physical deaths. God left His postmarks of soft angel's wings for a little boy, an angel's hand print on a man's shoulder, a vision of a recently deceased daughter, and a miraculous healing for others so we could see Him at work in the midst of tragedy.

God knows what it is like to lose an only Son. He aches with us. He hurts with us. He would allow death to come "too soon" to a loved one who belongs to Him only when His glory is in residence and His rescue for us is yet to be revealed. His gift of enlightenment will reveal this to us when we go home to be with Him.

God's Word is saturated with messages of how He is at work in our world today. Study it. Read it. Pray over it. His postmarks for your life are embedded there and waiting for your discovery. He is right beside you and preparing you for a blessing that will thrill your soul! Praise Him! Praise Him!

God's postmarks for your life are embedded in His Word. Read it, study it, and pray over it!

Sorrow Came to Visit

Sorrow came to me and:

Knocked me down hard, but not out of God's soft grasp

Wrapped itself tightly around me, but it could not dwell inside of me where the Lord rests

Threatened to rob me of the pleasures from this world, but it could not steal the joy of the Lord that permeates my soul

Stole my moments of light heartedness and laughter to be substituted by God's gift of eternal light

Tried blinding me from seeing a vision of a shining future, but God shed His light on a path of victory for me

Counted my dwindling days of experiencing the fullness of life, to be replaced by God's promise of a heavenly restoration beyond all earthly possibilities

Brought lies about chance and luck as my masters, to be wiped out by a vision of God's hand on my life

Sorrow's allotted time will soon be vanquished by the living God as His purpose for me is accomplished. I wait in expectation for Him as I rejoice in His presence.

—Barbara Cornelius

Photo Gallery

Chapter 1
Martha Elizabeth Cornelius, age 3, named after my mother, Martha Spencer

Chapter 2
Brandon and Alyssa Wyatt inside a rainbow bubble

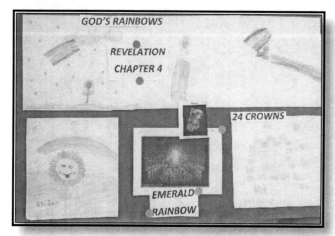

Rainbow illustrations for a lesson on Chapter 4 Revelation by my granddaughter Jacie Snipes (age 7)

Chapter 3
Michael Williams assisting me in assembling plant science kits at his hardware store

Chapter 4
My daughter Jennifer (age 2) with her grandfather Melvin Cornelius

Chapter 7
Alyssa and the carousel horse

Alyssa crying with Santa

**Chapter 9
My wonderful friend
Gloria Parker**

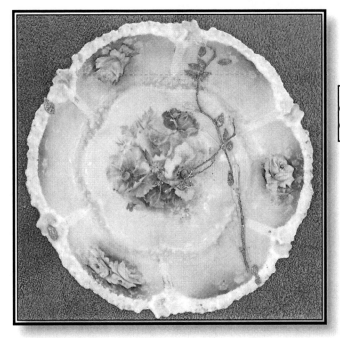

**Chapter 10
Great Aunt Ida's
dish after repair**

Chapter 13
The beautiful throw made from scraps; my cousin (sister) Mary Dell Memering and me

Chapter 14
My hometown church—The Carbon Methodist Church

Chapter 18
My "dead" tree a
few months before it
broke into pieces.

My brother Bobby's house slippers, ball, and coloring book

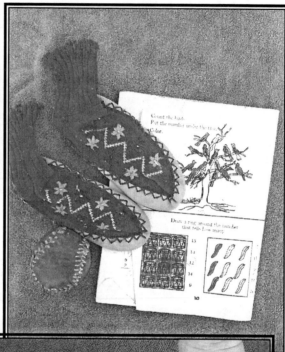

My Grandmother Overstreet and her rolling pin

Chapter 21
My grandchildren, back row, L to R: Brandon Wyatt, Alyssa Wyatt
front row, L to R: Benjamin Snipes, Jacie Snipes

Chapter 22
My "hearty" poinsettia plants in my sunroom

A Family Prayer

Dear Heavenly Father,

Track down every member of our extended family and bring into captivity their every thought, so they will have a heart to belong to You. Breathe on each of them and place Your healing power inside them, releasing them from any brokenness and pain that is suffocating their spirit.

Let everyone in our family be so filled with Your love that they pass Your light to a thousand generations! Let every generation of our family have people who share Your Word, Your Truth, and Your Way!

∼Amen

Exodus 20:6

"I lavish unfailing love for a thousand generations on those who love me and obey my commands."

Cornelius Family, Christmas 2013
L to R, back row: Alyssa Wyatt, Julie Cornelius with Jeffrey Cornelius, Brandon Wyatt, Benjamin Snipes, Earl Snipes, Robert Cornelius, Jennifer Snipes
L to R, front row: Abigail Cornelius, Jeff Cornelius, Martha Cornelius, Barbara Cornelius, Larry Cornelius, Jacie Snipes

Author's Closing Note:

Four years ago, when I was writing my first book, *Lazarus Still Rises*, a friend gave me a copy of the book *Two Sons Twice Born* by Hilda Atkins Moore. My friend personally knew Hilda, and said she might be open to speaking with me and providing guidance about the process of self-publishing my book.

When I called Hilda, she invited my husband and me to come visit her, and this was the beginning of my finding the Lord's footprints for my life as a Christian author. Hilda's testimony in her book blessed and inspired me to write about the ways the Lord had touched my life. She is a remarkable lady, and the countenance of the Lord is on her as she seeks to give Him honor and glory. I am eternally grateful for her love and guidance, and I seek to pass this blessing on to others as the Lord orders my steps.

After meeting the author and her husband, I was impressed and knew her book would bring a larder of inspirational food to many. During and after reading *Lazarus Still Rises*, my heart and soul were moved deeply by her memorial stone messages. This book is especially for those who are struggling with their spiritual lives, but who of us no longer needs encouragement? Ms. Cornelius uses her personal experiences of faith and miracles in a down-to-earth way that allows each reader's spirit to feel our merciful Lord's amazing grace.

〜Hilda Moore
Two Sons Twice Born

About The Author

Barbara Cornelius grew up in the small town (population 500) of Carbon, Indiana. She was blessed to be raised in a Christian family who were members of the Carbon United Methodist Church. For the past thirty years, Barbara, has been a member of the Tuckston United Methodist Church in Athens, Georgia. Being surrounded by so many people who walked in an intimate relationship with the Lord has given Barbara insight to recognize some of the numerous ways God daily reveals signs of His presence.

Having been a classroom teacher for thirty-seven years has also given Barbara many opportunities to see the hand of God work on behalf of those who seek Him and His presence in their lives.

Married for forty eight years to Larry Cornelius, she also has two adult children and eight grandchildren. She considers them the true prosperity and treasure of her life, given to her by the living God.

Barbara has also written another book: *Lazarus Still Rises.* This book gives true stories of faith and miracles that she has witnessed in the lives of God's people.

CPSIA information can be obtained at www.ICGtesting.com
Printed in the USA
LVOW13s0057160614

390182LV00002B/6/P